UNDERSTANDING THE
LEARNING DISABLED ATHLETE

UNDERSTANDING THE LEARNING DISABLED ATHLETE

A Guide for
Parents, Coaches, and Professionals

By

ANDREW GARY YELLEN, Ph.D.

and

HEIDI LAUREN YELLEN, M.A., C.E.T.

CHARLES C THOMAS • PUBLISHER
Springfield • Illinois • U.S.A.

Published and Distributed Throughout the World by
CHARLES C THOMAS • PUBLISHER
2600 South First Street
Springfield, Illinois 62794-9265

© *1987 by* CHARLES C THOMAS • PUBLISHER
ISBN 0-398-05316-2
Library of Congress Catalog Card Number: 86-30216

With THOMAS BOOKS *careful attention is given to all details of manufacturing
and design. It is the Publisher's desire to present books that are satisfactory as to their
physical qualities and artistic possibilities and appropriate for their particular use.*
THOMAS BOOKS *will be true to those laws of quality that assure a good name
and good will.*

Printed in the United States of America
Q-R-3

Library of Congress Cataloging in Publication Data

Yellen, Andrew Gary.
    Understanding the learning disabled athlete.

    Bibliography: p.
    Includes index.
    1. Sports for the handicapped. 2. Learning
disabilities. I. Yellen, Heidi Lauren. II. Title.
GV709.3.Y34   1987   796'.01'96   86-30216
ISBN 0-398-05316-2

ABOUT THE AUTHORS

ANDREW G. YELLEN, Ph.D. — Dr. Yellen practices in Clinical and Sports Psychology in Los Angeles, California and is also with the Los Angeles Unified School District. He holds Bachelor's and Master's degrees in physical education and a Doctorate in Clinical Psychology. He has been in education for seventeen years, and for fifteen years he was the head swimming coach and football coach at Grant High School in the Los Angeles City Schools. Dr. Yellen credits many of his colleagues, former students, and former athletes for the knowledge he has gained over the years by sharing their psychological, personal, and athletic problems with him. It is from this perspective that he approaches sports psychology and the learning disabled athlete.

HEIDI L. YELLEN, M.A., C.E.T. — Mrs. Yellen is in private practice in Los Angeles, California, and is a Certified Professional member of the Association of Educational Therapists. She is also with the Los Angeles Unified School District. She holds a Bachelor's degree in elementary education, a Master's degree in Counseling, and is a registered Psychometrist, Learning Handicapped Specialist, and Resource Specialist, dealing with children and adults with learning difficulties. Mrs. Yellen has been in education for seventeen years and has worked with the learning disabled for the last thirteen years. She is an educational consultant to a number of private schools. Her diagnostic and remediating abilities have earned her the respect of many of the educational institutions and private psychologists and psychiatrists in the Los Angeles area.

Together, the Yellens give a novel perspective with which to manage the learning disabled athlete. Their combined years of empirical observation and diligent efforts furnish the reader with more than theoretical ideas. They have given the professional and the layperson a thorough understanding of learning disabilities as they relate to athletics and have provided methods for remediation, compensation, and practical application of the knowledge gained.

This book is dedicated to our children, Joshua and Erit

PREFACE

THIS BOOK is intended to serve as a guideline for parents, coaches, and all professionals working with athletes. It creates a basis for awareness and further research and knowledge in the field of the learning disabled athlete. When exploring the related literature in cognition, academic learning disabilities, psychometric testing, and socialization, one sees that there has been no exploration of learning disabilities in athletics. By underscoring the disabilities manifest in sport and the need for remediation and compensation, a previously unrecognized problem is exposed so that it may be dealt with on a meaningful professional level.

With new laws passed for support and restructuring of curricula for special education, much attention has been focused upon learning disabilities and the attempts to provide an individualized education program (IEP) to meet the needs of these people. Yet nothing has been done to develop guidelines to assist those working with the learning disabled athletes in a sports-oriented environment. Many derogatory terms have been ascribed to young people who simply could not learn what a coach or instructor had to offer. After fifteen years as a coach, one of the authors has concluded that a more significant portion of the athletic population than previously believed has a disability that did not allow them to fully comprehend the concepts, rules, and actions being taught in the conventional manner. Therefore, a strong need exists to ensure that the learning disabled athlete is provided with an atmosphere conducive to better performance.

Along with relating learning disabilities specifically to athletics, the authors cite examples to illustrate the disabilities in the context of performance. Case histories are discussed to evaluate practical application of the information examined. The story of his personal struggle with a learning disability is told by Bruce Jenner, 1976 Olympic Gold Medal Decathlete, in his own words. Additional coping strategies are discussed so that practical application of the knowledge gained may be undertaken immediately.

Much of what has been discussed and recommended is based upon empirical observation and needs to be modified for the particular individual and sport. Insightful and thorough research is needed to refine the process and meet the needs of the learning disabled athlete.

ACKNOWLEDGMENTS

IT IS WITH gratefulness and love that we wish to acknowledge the following people for their contributions to our efforts. We hope that all who endeavor to create have such a support group.

To Drs. Sally and Michael Rabkin, thank you for helping prepare an environment for a new seed to grow. To Dr. James Gibbons and Dr. Nathalie Prettyman, thank you for your inspirations. To Sierra University, thank you for the environment. To "Tonto," thank you for all your efforts.

To our parents, thank you for the foundation. You have always been supportive through anything we endeavored.

To our children, Joshua and Erit, thank you for being understanding and supportive. Our desire to be the best possible role models was one of the driving forces behind this work.

And a special thanks to Bruce Jenner for sharing the private and difficult moments of his disability so that others may find the path easier.

CONTENTS

UNDERSTANDING THE
LEARNING DISABLED ATHLETE

Chapter One

INTRODUCTION

IN NO OTHER sphere of our culture is the fierceness of loyalties more apparent than in that of sport. For the individual, the path of athletics offers an opportunity to gain much positive notoriety. It is a small wonder that many are drawn to sport as a means of self-enhancement, self-identification, and social image. It is hoped that with a thorough understanding of the issues at hand, the parent, the coach, trainer, sports psychologist, and others who may work closely with these people may be receptive to new ideas in dealing with these individuals.

To the learning disabled individual the avenue of athletics offers something even greater. It offers an avenue of success. Yet, the very same limitations that prevent that person from achieving in a fully academic atmosphere hinder the athletic development. They do so not through the actual skills but rather through the inability of the person to absorb the necessary information to improve the quality of the performance. Here, talk is not of the severely handicapped individual but rather about that person whose skills have brought them to a significant point in their athletic endeavors. They have been labelled by Kranes the "Marginally Learning Disabled."

> They look and sound normal, but they feel shunned, isolated, and tormented. Their IQ's are in the 75 to 95 range, and it is estimated that they represent approximately 15 percent of our population. They have been referred to as "borderline," as "slow learners," as "exceptional"—but they are the Marginally Learning Disabled . . . our "shadow children" who are, in many ways, the loneliest group of people in the world (52).

In the field of athletics many have long called these individuals "uncoachable." The stereotype is usually quite clear. There is a fair amount, and in many cases a high degree, of natural talent present. Allowed to perform on their own, the athlete exhibits tremendous potential. The coach then attempts to improve the skills of the individual and to mold them to fit into a particular system. Something does not mesh, and the budding athlete is labelled with such terms as "lazy, not dedicated, too good to have to learn, selfish, irresponsible," and numerous other detrimental concepts. The majority of these stem from the frustrations of both the coach and athlete.

A concept that certainly needs to be studied more carefully is that the learning disabled youngster with skill, given no other means of positive reinforcement, gravitates to athletics because of the immediate gratification that can be gained from the activity. It has been an empirical observation over fifteen years of coaching experience and working with learning disabled youngsters that the percentage of marginally learning disabled people is greater in athletics than in the general population.

Today there is a great emphasis on providing an educational atmosphere to meet the needs of all individuals. Various states have enacted legislation to ensure that school districts are following guidelines necessary to enhance the potential of learning disabled youngsters. Yet, as stated before, many of these people do not qualify for special programs. And the area that literally no one has addressed is that of meeting the needs of the MLD athlete. It is relatively safe to state, after a rather thorough and complete search of available services, that the idea of addressing the needs of these athletes has not even been mentioned. The pertinent literature reviewed encompasses core areas of cognition, learning disabilities, psychometric testing, and socialization skills, but the issue of adapting these concepts to athletics is the central theme of the book.

One of the most difficult areas when dealing with an athlete is the concept of immediacy. For the average MLD individual, the remediation process can be quite lengthy, and, in fact, support may need to continue throughout the educational as well as professional time frame. Unfortunately, sport leaves little room for slow processes. The coaches know it, the support personnel know it, but most of all the athlete knows and is constantly given evidence that time is a critical factor in performance and the athletic cast system: first team, second team, third team, and no team. The person in golf, for instance, needs a simple and precise diagnosis and prescription so that he or she can walk immediately to the course and correct the problem. And in sports such as skiing or gymnastics such *instant cures* can literally make a difference between serious injury or death and an outstanding performance. For a matter of self-preservation, the athlete has learned to ignore long-term remedies and go with *results*.

The coaches are also involved in this area. Sport will never allow for the gradual process, and therefore, the people involved must adjust. It should be the objective of every coach to develop each person under his or her influence to full potential. The MLD athlete is not capable of making the necessary adjustments, and so the burden lays with the coach. One of the tenets of the communication process is that the burden of communication lays with the communicator, not the receiver. Emphasized in simplest terms, "If you want someone to do what you've said, you'd damned well better say it in a manner they can understand!" And this is precisely the underlying premise of this book. Let the sports arena eradicate the idea of the "lazy, undedicated, selfish, irresponsible, and uncoachable athlete" by addressing the issue in an academic fashion. The merits of sports programs on all levels are many and varied. It is time that it included the needs of the MLD individual, as well.

It is hoped that this work will provide impetus for much needed research in the field. Perhaps a new paradigm will be created with regard to the MLD athlete, beginning with the recognition that such an individual exists. It is also the hope of the authors that the information in the remainder of the book will be useful in working with all athletes, not only those with learning disabilities.

Chapter Two

BACKGROUND INFORMATION

IN ORDER TO fully understand the depth of the problem for the learning disabled athlete, a review of some background literature is in order. Here, the term *background* holds a special significance since there currently exists no body of knowledge in this area whose specificity sheds light on the subject matter. To be discussed are the areas of cognition, learning disabilities, psychometric testing, and socialization. While it may seem that some of the material discussed has no bearing upon the learning disabled athlete, it should be noted that the information provided allows a broad perspective with which to view the subject. One cannot fully understand the difficulties involved unless one understands the basis for the problems. Unfortunately, as shown repeatedly in the literature, learning disabled individuals are also plagued by a greater percentage of psychopathologies, obscuring the problem for those not familiar with the broad spectrum. Heretofore, no one has tied all the loose ends together.

COGNITION

"A cognitive theory is concerned especially with central organizing processes in higher animals, and it recognizes a partial autonomy of those processes, such that the animal becomes an actor on, rather than simply a reactor to, its environment (67:7)." That idea manifests itself as the central theme of the broad area of cognitive psychology. As the pinnacle of the evolutionary ladder, the human being does far more than merely wander through life in a passive fashion. Humankind impacts the world in a continuously changing fashion that precludes any thoughts of being merely a rung on that ladder.

Two thoughts come to mind as to why there is so numerous an amount of theories pertaining to thinking, cognition, and memory. The first may be that the relative recency of the study of cognitive psychology offers many more individuals an opportunity to explore its depths. A second, and perhaps more plausible, explanation lays with the concept that there is no complete understanding of how the functions actually occur, thereby leaving a vast area of conjecture. Educators continue to research and explore cognition, for if the secrets should be unlocked, the rapidity of learning becomes virtually limitless. The contributions of such notable figures as Luris and Piaget are certainly not to be discounted. Yet reality dictates that the following statement holds far greater credence than any current theory: "Nobody knows for sure how we know." That terse comment may be an oversimplification to some scholars of cognition, but upon a thorough examination of contemporary views in cognitive psychology, one cannot deny that a diversity, and quite often a polarity, of ideas exist. Each has a substantial body of research to validate the theory and to justify the conclusion. As Posner suggests in his book on cognition, "It has been difficult to design and execute experiments which reveal the basic mental operations underlying the myriad different kinds of thinking (70:10)."

If one begins to consider the areas of speech, reading, phonological coding, spelling, writing, object recognition, hypotheses testing, mathematics, search strategies, and problem solving, to name only several, then the realization of cognitive processes becomes much more than a simple branch of a larger body of knowledge. It becomes a complex body in its own right, with many subspecialties to be dealt with. Each of these has numerous theories proposed with good empirical evidence as their justification. To further complicate the situation, two more preconceptions begin to cloud the issues. First, there exists the possibility that knowledge and memory may be accomplished differently at different stages of life. Second, with the current research in right brain-left brain hypotheses, it appears that individuals may process the same information in different fashions.

The facts, though sometimes overwhelming, create, themselves, a new respect. With all the time, effort, and money invested, science can still not explain the almost magical part of each person.

It has been illustrated often that the clinician needs to have a broad familiarity with the theories of cognition. But objectivity dictates that psychology still be labelled a *trial and error* science until such time as the exact mechanisms can be isolated, researched, and explained. At that point, the function of the psychologist will be to pinpoint the faulty circuit board, and then to replace it, whether in a literal or figurative sense. In the meantime, it is this very abstract formation that continues to add to the fascination associated with the human mind. There are certainly those who believe that the *code* should never be broken. But curiosity about the very essence of life dictates a continued effort to understand the species.

And lest humankind become complacent with the body of knowledge, we must constantly reevaluate the position. Many of the theories currently discussed are based upon the principle of a biological clock, circadian rhythms, that have been widely accepted by scientists from a variety of disciplines. Recent tests of the manned space shuttle have thrown considerable doubt on the clock theory. The premise of circadian rhythms states that the time sequencing for living things is innate. Should the empirical observations of the space research be tested and proven valid, then it would create a new paradigm, resulting in the reorganization of many of the theories of cognition.

PIAGET

There are a considerable number of scholars who have contributed greatly to the field of cognitive psychology, but Piaget and his associates have accumulated the largest collection of factual and theoretical observation that exist today (68:3). From the hard core research and scientific community comes the major criticism of the works of Piaget. The assertion is that his theories are based solely on clinical experiences and observations as opposed to true scientific methodology. To many that very fact becomes an asset to his works rather than the assumed liability. Piaget's expressed concern was with people, and his realm of theories of cognition was more concerned with understanding the *how* of the reality than with prediction and control of individual behavior.

As Piaget explains the phenomenon of learning, adaptation is a biological function. A change in the structures constitutes *development*. This development encompasses much more than merely learning in a broad sense. His memory in the specific sense refers to the figurative aspect of remembering. But the "conservation of schemes," as it was labelled, involved a Gestalt rather than a simple memory.

One of the core ideas of the Piaget theories is that of equilibration. This equilibration is a process of attaining a homeostatic equilibrium between external intrusions and the activities of the internal organism. It is this idea of balance that forms the foundation for many of his other hypotheses.

Having spent a considerable portion of his life concerned with the child, Piaget considers five factors in the intellectual development of the child (22:31). First, maturation is simply the gradual unfolding of a genetic plan, whatever it might be. This, of course, would vary from one individual to another and would account for differences even within the nuclear family. Second, physical experience is the transfer of the contact with the physical world to the mind. In psychoanalytical terms this is the study of object relations. Third, logico-mathematical experience is the idea of constructing relationships between things. The extension of this would be called logical sequencing. Fourth, social transmission is the knowledge that is constructed from interactions with other people. This is the very issue that social psychologists deal with. And the fifth is the previously discussed equilibration.

The process is one of continual organization and reorganization integrating the previous one into itself. In essence, the organism is continuously creating a new paradigm in which to operate. Even though the process is continuous, Piaget holds that the results are discontinuous, being qualitatively different from time to time. Hence comes the idea that cognition may occur in a different manner at various chronological ages. Piaget breaks these down into periods and stages. The Sensorimotor Period from zero to two years is divided into six stages. From zero to one month is exercising the ready-made sensorimotor schemes. Everything is *getting in shape* to receive. One to four months is the primary circular reactions. Secondary circular reactions encompass four to eight months. From eight to twelve months is the coordination of secondary schemes. Twelve to eighteen months is tertiary circular reactions. And eighteen to twenty-four months is the invention of new means through mental combinations. The Preoperational Period is from two to seven years. The Concrete Operations Period is from seven to eleven years. And the final stage of child development culminates with the Formal Operations Period from eleven to fifteen years.

During the Sensorimotor Period one can follow interplay of assimilation and accommodation. Ths is also called the operative and figurative aspects of knowing. The individual advances from absorbing bits and pieces of information about the real world to symbolic thinking. The recognition of mother and father occurs during this phase. The *bonding* so frequently discussed in the literature occurs during this period.

The developing child enters the Preoperational Period. A more stable and cohesive world highlights this phase. The child can deal mentally with objects and events that are distant. The individual does not yet have full grasp of the relation of objects in his or her reality. These relations form the beginning of a concrete reality.

A great variety of cerebral operations mark Concrete Operations. Piaget suggests such concepts as decentering, reversibility, taking the view of others, etc. Adult time and pace reality are generally constructed at this time. The foundations for the next period of development are put in place.

In Formal Operations, the adolescent begins with the Concrete Operations, much like a lump of unsculpted clay. The Concrete Operations are molded and shaped to form a semipermanency. This gives rise to the impressionable child versus the dogmatic adult. He or she is testing out reality as it relates to formed ideas. These propositions then become an integral part of the individual's cognitive structure. This makes possible hypotheses that do not correspond to any particular experience. To the adult, this would account for some of the off-the-wall thought patterns associated with teenagers. At this stage of development the person can begin with the reality and check that reality against various memories of past experiences and against sensory feedback. The individual is then free to arrive at his or her own conclusions based upon the thought process.

It should be reiterated at this point that Piaget approached the situations more as an observer than as one who had the intent of theory formations (68:119). Much of his thinking has allowed those who deal with children to gain a fuller understanding of the developmental processes and, hence, improve the interaction with adults. At the same time it enables the clinician to gain insight into some adult problems that resulted from a disorder in childhood cognitive development.

LEARNING TO SPEAK

The human infant not only listens to sound but also produces sounds. Many have even suggested that a *silent sound* exists within the womb. The first recognized sound is that of the birth cry and for some period of time the crying is the only method of producing sound. Yet the mother is often able to distinguish different cries as representing different needs of the infant. The crying sounds consist of single vowels and consonants. All things being normal, the ability to hear sounds and to produce the sound elements of language is inborn. The infant must learn to produce the sound elements in specific patterns if a language is to be spoken. Since children learn to speak the language of the culture into which they were born, it seems evident that hearing is a necessary prerequisite for the normal sequence leading to language. This is evidenced by the difficulty in developing verbal function and thought processes in hearing impaired children (31:63).

Generally speaking, words are learned within a behavioral context. The child begins to associate behavioral actions with specific words. This is an important concept to consider at any level of education. For the child's language behavior to have a symbolic function, the child must eventually learn to respond to a spoken word by some behavior other than imitating the word. One often overlooked aspect of problems is the ability to transfer words to symbols.

A basic factor in the learning process is the child himself. It must be assumed that vocal behavior is an inborn response to both internal and external stimuli (48:26). This is evidenced by the myriad ways that an infant plays with his or her voice. These stimuli produce vocal behavior which, in turn, produce vocal behavior on the part of the parents or others. These interactions appear to satisfy the child's needs. The child's behavior becomes organized relative to objects to means of verbal cues.

The words used by the child and others become integral parts of behavior patterns. The underlying premise is that the language plays a much greater role in total behavior development than that of a simplified component (55:137).

The development process begins with a few words and a number of stimuli to which the child responds with either words or preverbal sounds. An observer can tell the difference from one behavior to another, and the child can recognize similarities between one situation and another. In this way, the coos, gurgles, and words become associated with particular behaviors. The child is able to distinguish differences by utilizing various criteria.

New but somewhat familiar situations bring forth similar verbal response. As the stimuli become more intricate the child is able to distinguish in greater detail. In this way, a solid foundation is then built upon. The end result will be new words with greater clarifying characteristics.

But alas, for all the literature that theorizes how a child learns to read, including discussions on coding, graphics, structure, thought processes, etc., there exists one very observable conclusion. To date, no one really knows. From psychologists to neurologists to educators, there exists no precise explanation on how the normal individual learns to read (85:197).

Memory

The process of memory may be divided into three systems (9:38). The first is an instant memory that holds things for a few seconds. For instance, the remembering of a phone number just long enough to dial it would constitute instant memory. The second is classified as short-term memory which includes a small number of things that are active at the conscious level at any one specific time. Auditory and visual sequencing are examples of short-term memory. The remainder of all things stored is long-term memory. It is also possible to distinguish between the three qualitatively different memory codes: imagery; enactive; and symbolic. Each of these provides the individual with different types of information.

Instant memory appears to act more like a bridge from one area to another. The information in instant memory is certainly important for normal functioning, but acts as a transitional mode rather than a separate entity.

Active memory is used both to try out new organizational patterns of thoughts on a temporary basis and to organize the storage of information in long-term memory. It has been described as the work desk with which to organize material going into a file cabinet. This is generally accomplished relating incoming and retrieved experience within the same temporal memory cells. It is also used to sustain experience long enough to allow various mental operations to code or file experience within different categories.

Long-term memory is a constantly changing entity in the sense that it is subject to reorganization by new memory cells. There are those who hypothesize that forgetting, excluding injury to brain tissue, does not mean that information is no longer present. It rather signifies a weakness in the retrieval system. Hypnotherapy and hypnotism would tend to validate this hypothesis (41:82).

The retrieval process can be divided into two parts. Retrieval occurs with little or no effort when input contacts the proper area with no conscious search. Harder retrieval comes about when an individual is forced to look for information or cannot find the information stored in long-term memory. Ambiguous stimuli can also result in this process. In simplest terms, the pondering of a question would be classified as retrieval with effort.

Interestingly, these previously discussed concepts became the key to the synthetic modern brain, the computer. Words on the monitor are the instant memory, appearing and disappearing at very short intervals. The ROM and RAM are the short-term memory, acting as the work table. The discs then become the long-term memory, including programs. How ironic that the very mechanism that, as experts say, does or will run every aspect of our lives is modeled after the human brain. And when people like d'Ydevalle (30:118) tell us that we are using only about one tenth of our brain potential, the complexity of the mind can be somewhat ascertained.

SYMBOLIC CONCEPTS

The human mind has the ability to go beyond individual objects and produce a more general system for the classification of information. Recognizing and identifying concepts may be divided into two parts. The first is learning the fields or attributes that pertain to the classification. The second is learning the classification rules which allow varying information or circumstances to be assigned to a particular category. Many of the concepts that we develop come from a passive behavior. We also form hypotheses which allow us to test the rules by which we categorize against the examples provided by experience, what psychologists call reality testing. The last concept of reality testing either validates or nullifies the hypothesis.

It should be apparent that memory structures which underlie human cognition are complicated, to say the least. Many of the same processes involved in symbolic concept development are also involved in judgment (22:84).

Attributes are suggested by the structure of a problem and the subsequent variety of instances with which an individual is provided. Attention is drawn to particular attributes and these are then the deciding factors in a judgment. The idea that experience is important underscores the notion that the more one has to draw from in terms of attributes, the more precise the judgment (53:208). The tendency of individuals to only use a small number of attributes with which they are comfortable leads to oversimplification of decision making. In simplest terms this is labelled as narrow-mindedness.

In many ways educators use this process to assist learning. Not only are ideas discussed, but categorization; i.e., the outline, is also taught so that future judgments in need of this information are adequately supplied.

MENTAL OPERATIONS

Mental operations require a varying degree of time. These are directly relative to the complexity of the process. However, in the case of abstract reasoning, many different operations may overlap. A single experience may at once be part of auditory associations and part of associations to verbal descriptions. The overlapping process may be true for a number of different combinations. The degree to which either is emphasized depends on the last set of circumstances. In this case circumstances is reality, both internal and external. Experiments indicate that visual and linguistic associations are separable processes in the nervous system, even though they overlap in time. In simplest terms, the mind is capable of many operations simultaneously in an amazingly accurate fashion. The more that medical science discovers about the human mind, the more complex and capable it appears. Furthermore, much of this can be improved through the process that has come to be called education (76:121).

Material may be activated either by external stimulation or by internal instruction. This idea relates back to Piaget's concept of equilibration, that the individual blends internal and external forces. Internal stimulation requires considerable time. This is particularly true when it involves visual imagining brought about from a verbal instruction. This material can be brought to active memory to be worked out and reworked. The amount of time for the process to take place will be a direct result of a number of items that need to be integrated into the process. As a result, internal ideas are used to look at reality, and reality is used to evaluate internal ideas.

At this level, complex tasks such as meaningful interpersonal relationships can be broken down into an orderly set of operations. As was the case in the prior situation, the time required to complete any of these tasks is directly dependent upon the number of steps required to simplify the task. What the individual learns from the whole process is called problem solving. The problem is first broken down into component parts which can be more readily managed. Basically speaking, the whole is disassembled, the individual parts are examined and comprehended. Then the parts are reassembled, and the whole can be fully comprehended.

PROBLEM SOLVING

Thought is the continuing process of achieving new configurations and representations through the functioning performance of mental operations (85:192). Experiences are added to memory broadening the foundation with which to analyze new situations. If these operations are under the general guidance of a conscious plan, that is to say the mental operations are systematic, then the thought is organized. This may be a self-learned or taught skill. However, when the mental operations follow no specific pattern, are unrelated, or chosen with no reference to a plan, then the thought is similar to daydreaming. Even a think tank, in which new ideas are discussed in a random fashion in an attempt to evoke a new concept, attacks the situation in an orderly fashion. Random ideas attached to nothing remain as random ideas. While either may be on the conscious level, the organized pattern gives a subjective effect of considerable effort. And it certainly requires more time and mental effort, but it is this type of thought that leads to efficient problem solving. The teaching of problem solving abilities is a prime concern among educators.

Individuals are continuously faced with an incredible amount of problems. These problems vary not only quantitatively but qualitatively, that is to say that many are more intense (55:231). The key elements as to whether or not an effective solution will be found are twofold. The first stage will be how the initial problem is perceived. The second will be the systematic influence of a plan on all subsequent mental operations. It is interesting that in order to overcome limitations of memory, people tend to return frequently to the starting position. As an example, when one forgets where something was placed, a common strategy is to physically go back and retrace all the steps leading to the disappearance. This same simplistic method is employed even at sophisticated levels of criminology. It is almost as though the mind has the ability to retrace the exact nerve pathways leading to memory as the body retraces the physical pathways.

The search phase of mental operations may be quite effortless and unconscious. This special characteristic gives rise to reports of problem solving during a period of rest or sleep. Many individuals report working through problems during sleep that had previously confounded all attempts. A pad and pencil or tape recorder next to the bed are ways of saving the solution upon arising. This phenomenon is, perhaps, a result of clearing the mind and being able to work without distractions. Sensory input has been turned to its lowest level and the mind is clear to work from an internal stimulus position.

Problem solving, as previously stated, is certainly a trainable skill. Educators are realizing that just as mathematics, science, language, and other disciplines are encountered, so should problem solving be included. If one considers many of the problems encountered by the clinician, from a cognitive viewpoint, the number of psychological difficulties stemming from poor problem solving abilities is considerable.

From a practical sense, there is no concrete application of the cognitive aspects discussed. It is more abstract organization. From the scientific viewpoint, "If it can't be observed and recorded, it is worthless." Yet, perhaps a new paradigm is under construction. Many of the tools of the psychologist include abstracts such as intuition. The importance of cognitive psychology is that clinicians recognize the various components of the mental processes. Even if specific theories are not universally accepted, there still exists a general body of knowledge from which to draw.

It is noteworthy to mention that teaching models and computers are modeled after the human cognitive process, even though it is not fully understood.

LEARNING DISABILITIES

Of all the areas in which most clinical psychologists are the least proficient, learning disabilities would certainly stand at the top of the list. Perhaps it is because most clinicians view this area as one to be handled by an educational psychologist or some other branch of the discipline. Even the clinical licensure examination does not require a significant display of knowledge in this area. And yet, upon further investigation, one usually finds an individual, as well as the nuclear family, in stress as a result of a learning disability. It has even been noted that these same clinically significant problems arose due to either an intentional or unintentional lack of recognition of that disability. With updated resources and sophisticated computer cross-referenced research, criminologists have discovered a high correlation between those who perpetrate crimes upon society and those who have learning disabilities. It is only because of the numerous studies that have dealt with the total psychological picture of the individual that some clinicians are beginning to focus in on this problem that plagues a much greater portion of society than what was formerly realized.

Unfortunately, the idea that a learning disability can fall into a simple diagnosis and prognosis is very inaccurate. Even in this technological age with the use of magnetic resonance imagery (MRI) and positron emission tomography (PET) which give us the ability to view the brain at work, the so-called experts are still not precisely sure how the brain functions and how the human being learns. And it is only after these processes are identified that malfunctions in the form of learning disabilities may be understood. It is only recently that the government has mandated help for the learning disabled students by having resource specialists to handle specific problems. Because of its recency the position is left unfilled in many districts throughout the country. Educational therapy is still not considered a complete major in many institutions of higher learning. Progress is being made to have more specialists, as well as to educate the average teacher with regard to the particular needs of these individuals. It should be noted that most educators have little or no knowledge about learning disabilities. This is most certainly due to the lack of preparation by institutions training our educators and does not reflect on the dedication of the teachers themselves. Equally important is providing a service in conjunction with the specialists and to educate with regard to understanding exactly what a learning disability encompasses.

As stated previously, there is virtually no material written with regard to learning disabilities as they relate to athletics. Hence, a thorough comprehension of background information is vital to understanding the process.

The need for focusing on the remediation of learning disabilities as they relate to athletics has been established. No one yet has prescribed methods of aiding the *uncoachable* individual who has happened to sneak by on his or her skills alone.

Intervention in all aspects of the person's life is essential. The same basic concepts apply on and off the field. Since, in many cases, the coach is often the closest meaningful person to the athlete, why not provide the coach with the necessary tools to help the total individual, with auxiliary support from the resource specialist, educational psychologist and the clinician? This idea encompasses one of the major issues in sports psychology.

SPECIFIC DISABILITIES

Rather than placing a specific label on a disability, the current trend is to identify the disability by its effect upon the individual. The rationalization for this is to place the emphasis on the remediation and compensation with a return to a functional level, rather than being bogged down with the nomenclature of diagnosis. Certainly such terms as dyslexia or dyscalculia are to be discussed, but they have been replaced in many instances by discussions about problems in grammatic and auditory closure, attention deficit disorders (ADD), or visual memory problems. This entire process signifies the shift from identifying to remediating and compensating.

The skills involved in the development of the individual form a convenient check list of the clinician dealing with and attempting to pinpoint a learning disability. These are gross motor development, sensory motor integration, auditory skills, visual skills, language development, conceptual skills, and social skills.

Gross Motor Development

The term gross motor development refers to activities in which large muscle groups are utilized without the need to process external stimuli. Generally included is a list of skills that pertain to gross motor development: rolling, crawling, walking, running, throwing, jumping, and skipping. The actual physiological differentiation lies with the ratio of motor neurons to muscle fibers, thereby facilitating a finer and smoother movement. This allows for the differential applications of the terms gross and fine motor movement. In addition, the individual is able to identify body parts and has some degree of cross transference. Blockage of bilateral transference is one of the telltale signs of some type of interference in normal neural transmission. An evaluation of strength, flexibility, and endurance would also be included under this heading.

The problems normally associated with gross motor development are generally given the classification of "uncoordinated individual." The person does not possess the fluidity of movement associated with norms for the maturational level. Being a nonacademic area, this category is usually not accorded a tremendous amount of significance for the individual in terms of remediation. As a general rule, it is not often dealt with in a psychological arena. Yet, in the early developmental years as described by Piaget, it can lead to serious problems in social acceptance. Many young people gather their self-images from what occurs on the playground. Consider the child who is constantly picked last on a team, or worse, not picked at all.

Sensory Motor Integration

In laymen's terms this category is normally termed "eye-hand coordination." In the hierarchy of cognition and academia, it is considered only slightly more significant than gross motor development because of its relationship to stimuli processing. Areas of sensory motor integration include balance and rhythm, spatial awareness (kinesthetic sense), reaction-speed dexterity, tactile discrimination (which include the feel of actually performing a task), directionality (of which dyslexia is the most well-known malfunction), laterality (hand, eye, and foot), and time orientation.

In the area of sensorimotor integration, the clinician is concerned with the relationship between motor coordination and its neural coordinates for processing stimuli. The inability to strike a moving object, the inability to throw and hit an object, and the continual bumping into objects (i.e., "I was walking along minding my own business when the chair jumped out and hit me.") are three examples of sensorimotor integration. Whether a true processing problem or inability to perform the correct movements, the results are the same. Because of this, they should be dealt with in the same remedial fashion.

Auditory Skills

The first of four areas most often dealt with is auditory skills. Included under this heading are auditory acuity, auditory decoding, auditory-vocal association, auditory memory, and auditory sequencing.

Auditory acuity is the ability to receive and differentiate auditory stimuli. Here, as in other areas of learning disabilities, there may be several factors contributing to a deficit in auditory acuity. These range from a simple fluid buildup in the middle ear and Eustachian tube to severe auditory nerve impairment. Since the resultant problem is remediated in the same fashion from a therapist's perspective, not a medical perspective, to spend valuable time searching for a specific label is not in the best interest of the individual and, therefore, serves no useful purpose. A variety of listening skill development programs are used.

Decoding refers to the ability to understand sounds or spoken words. The individual who is free from impairment can follow simple verbal instructions and can indicate, whether verbally or nonverbally, the purpose or meaning of auditory stimuli. Carrying out a specific verbal command is an example of this skill. Certainly one of the most important tasks that an individual must learn is to follow verbal instructions, as well as understand questions. Before any judgment is made with regard to the quality of a particular answer, the therapist needs to be sure that the question was understood.

The ability to respond verbally in a meaningful fashion to auditory stimuli is referred to as auditory-vocal association. Sentence completion requires an understanding of the spoken word and some cognition so that a response is deemed correct. Identification of opposites and the relating of particular incidents in response to interrogation are also examples of this auditory skill. Of course, logic and sound judgment also play a role. In some instances the lack of understanding jokes or humorous situations may be an indication of a disability in the particular area rather than the traditional label of a poor sense of humor.

Auditory memory is defined as the ability to retain and to recall auditory stimuli. Along the auditory continuum an individual should be able to remember nursery rhymes, sing songs, or repeat the previous day's experiences. While most tests are written, which is a completely separate skill, most classroom activities involve auditory memory skills by participation in classroom discussions. Remembering correct grammatical usage in the classroom often plays a significant role in the teacher's determination of future grades.

Auditory sequencing is actually an extension of the previously discussed category of auditory memory. The individual must recall, in correct sequence and detail, prior auditory information. Exactly following sequential directions is an integral part of the entire educational experience. The repetition of digit and letter series are prerequisites to arithmetic and reading.

Visual Skills

The second major area to be delt with is that of visual skills. These include visual acuity, visual coordination and pursuit (sometimes called tracking), visual-form discrimination, visual figure-ground differentiation, visual memory, visual-motor memory, visual-motor fine muscle coordination, visual-motor spatial-form manipulation, visual-motor speed of learning, and visual-motor integration.

Visual acuity is the ability to see and to differentiate meaningfully and accurately in one's visual field. This is fully inclusive of an entire medical specialty, that of ophthalmology. Most people, however, consider the Snellen eye chart as a major indicator of visual acuity. Corrective lenses are the simplest way to effect change in the acuity of the individual. Good development should include visual exploration, description, and interpretation. The eyes, like other parts of the anatomy, will function better having been exposed to a variety of situations necessary for visual adaptation.

Visual coordination and pursuit, tracking, is the ability to follow and track objects and symbols with coordinated eye movement. The normal individual is able to fixate on stable objects and to follow moving objects without jerky movements. Training should consist of both general eye coordination movements, as well as specific directional training. Almost all sports skills require a sophisticated degree of visual tracking.

Visual-form discrimination is a form of decoding. It is the ability to visually differentiate the forms and symbols in one's environment. The usual criterion is the ability to match identical pictures and symbols such as numbers, words, letters, and abstract design. This skill is an absolute prerequisite to reading. The dyslexic individual has problems with differentiation to the point of severe disruption of the reading process. Oftentimes the best method of remediation is to begin the reading process again, much as it was in the primary grades. The skill of visual figure-ground differentiation is the ability to perceive objects in foreground and background and to separate them in a meaningful fashion. A properly developed individual should be able to pick out a particular person in a group picture or to find simple forms or words imbedded in other pictures or phrases. This skill encompasses visual scanning, peripheral discrimination, detection of significant details, and kinesthetic motor activities such as hitting a tennis ball or hitting a baseball with the bat.

Being able to accurately recall the specifics from prior visual experience is visual memory. The individual that excels at this skill is often said to have a photographic mind. The disabled individual has difficulty recognizing things that have changed in the environment and does not respond well to visual cues. This oftentimes is the skill that enables the running back to pick his way through a series of defenders. This, too, is in a progression of skills leading up to the ability to read. The steps involved are simple recall, symbol training, and word and number training.

Visual-motor memory is the ability to reproduce, motor-wise, prior visual experiences. Rather than merely identify, the individual should have the ability to draw designs and symbols, culminating with writing skills. More than merely writing, many individuals learn by imitating. Without this skill things must be constantly relearned. A person deficient in this area will have an extremely difficult time in the educational process.

As opposed to gross motor tasks, visual-motor fine muscle coordination is a higher neurological function. Fine eye-hand tasks, threading a needle as an example, require practice. Teachers utilize tracing and cutting among other things to develop this skill in youngsters. This is usually begun at about kindergarten age. The normal eye-hand coordination tasks also fall into this category. Though discussed in the sensorimotor area, this specific aspect discussed involves the visual modality.

To move in space and to manipulate three-dimensional materials is referred to as visual-motor spatial-form manipulation. The aptitude for building block houses or drawing three-dimensional pictures accurately are examples of this skill. Driving would be virtually impossible without mastery of this skill. Once again, for the athlete, this is a very necessary skill to achieve a superior performance.

There is significant evidence that the speed of learning can be greatly increased by repetitive skill work in the area of visual-motor speed of learning. The goal here is to turn the skill into a useful function. Sorting and copying are generally used for basic exercises to develop the skill, but can also be used for remediation.

Finally, visual motor integration is the knack for integrating total visual-motor skills in complex problem solving. A myriad of activities, including not only sports but music, art, and others, require a full integration of all elements previously discussed. Those activities in themselves provide ample opportunity for a person to practice these skills. For the athlete, the lack of ability in any one of these areas creates an almost insurmountable obstacle to superior performance.

Language Development

An individual's language development is the third area considered when discussing learning disabilities. The language development area encompasses the subcategories of vocabulary, fluency and encoding, articulation, word attack skills, reading comprehension, writing, and spelling.

Simply stated, vocabulary is one's ability to understand words. The clinical assessment is most often evaluated in terms of comparable chronological age and educational experience. The norming has been well established for vocabulary. Neurological integration and experience are responsible for development. However, even with the extent of current research there still appears no precise explanation. This skill of one's vocabulary is most often developed in three phases. A jargon, or simple imitative phase, is the most basic level of communication. For the most part, an individual at the earliest age is imitating sounds and words rather than cognitively expressing them. The second is a pragmatic phase that allows the person to function in everyday situations. Many people who lack full education have progressed no further than the pragmatic phase. Street languages would certainly fall into this area. The third is a symbolic phase which is a more complex procedure. The words at this point are sometimes labelled a more *sophisticated* vocabulary. They appear to require more cognitive processing than the pragmatic phase words.

Fluency and encoding are terms directed toward describing the ability to express oneself verbally. Such factors as fluency, lack of hesitation, and complex sentence structure are guidelines for determination of normalcy. This is to say that the verbal process should smooth out so that the words flow. For the impaired individual each word is an effort. It has been determined that a significant criterion for development of this skill is verbal stimulation. Considering this factor, a child's background will have much to do with abilities in this area. The child from the highly educated family is going to have a qualitatively higher degree of stimulation than the child from a poorly educated home and background.

Certainly an outgrowth of fluency and encoding, articulation connotes an individual's ability to pronounce words clearly without notable problems. The difficulties in articulation are generally classified as initial, medial, and final sounds. From a practical standpoint the presenting problem may be one of any combination of these three. Many parents concerned by articulation problems at an early age are simply not aware of the sounds considered normal for the various ages such as blends. Forcing the child to pronounce sounds which are beyond the capabilities may produce anxiety which may further inhibit proper articulation. A good portion of the problems disappear with age and maturity. An articulation problem still in evidence by the middle of the primary grades is noteworthy, and remediation may be in order.

A child's word attack skills are the ability to analyze words phonetically. This includes proper association, being able to break down words, and being able to recognize component words. Word attack skills are most often subdivided into vowels, consonants, blends, and combinations. There are certain rules and *tricks* that children are taught to aid in the process.

One of the most tested skills in higher education is that of reading comprehension. Reading comprehension is the ability to understand what one has read. Reading speed is certainly an asset but is virtually useless without the skill of comprehension. Comprehension must not be sacrificed for speed. A person should be able to recall and paraphrase a story and should further be able to attribute meaning to what was read. The levels of progression include assessment of individual words, sentence comprehension, paragraph comprehension, and story comprehension. The educator will note that this is the precise order of teaching composition skills.

Though the majority of human communication in everyday life is verbal, the ability to express oneself through written language is a tremendously important skill. The normal, educated person is able to communicate ideas through paragraph, letter, story, or essay. This skill is an integration which requires higher neurological functions, including visual-motor performance. Development usually begins with the training of hand muscle, tracing, and, finally, copying and independent writing. This particular area has been of great concern recently since the quality produced by those having finished their education is markedly inferior to previous groups. A major push for improvement in composition skills has taken place nationwide over the last two years.

Oftentimes the therapist hears, "But I'm just not a good speller." Spelling includes the written and oral modes. An individual should be able to spell within an accepted age and educational experience level. A useful subsequent result of proper spelling habits is the progression to more complex words. The skill of spelling is not rote exercise as some would have us believe.

Conceptual Skills

Although many consider only arithmetic skills in the conceptual category, it includes more. Areas of concentration to be considered are numbers concept, arithmetic process, arithmetic reasoning, general information, classification, and comprehension.

Numbers concept is the ability to count and to use simple numbers to represent quantity. Such skills as counting forward or backward, counting by twos, or grouping by quantities are considered objectives in this skill development. Three subareas usually practiced are the concept of more and less, number association and mixed sets, and advanced grouping. This skill is the basis for all other arithmetic techniques. As such, proficiency is of utmost importance prior to any progression. Many conceptual problems are a result of a poor foundation in numbers concept. It should be remembered that in many cases the arithmetic process is the training ground for the entire conceptual process and not merely in numbers.

The skills of adding, subtracting, multiplying and dividing are collectively labelled arithmetic process. Achievement tests attempt to classify an individual in comparison to others in the same chronological age. In a sense, this skill is the practical application of numbers concept. Arithmetic reasoning is the practical application of arithmetic process in problem solving. Such everyday use as purchasing goods, counting change, and weighing objects are included. Most definitely the educational process should include application to life skills. A large portion of time is spent dealing with money problems since, after all, it consumes a large part of our lives. For many in athletics a good portion of thought is related to numbers and statistics.

Part of the area of conceptual skills also includes the ability to acquire and utilize information from both education and experience. World problems, geography, national and local developments are all areas considered important because the individual must process the information and gain the ability to conceptualize from that information. It is the person, traditionally labelled narrow, who is generally void of such skill. In addition, a good portion of social judgment is predicated upon this skill. This means that along with affecting the conceptual process of the individual, it greatly affects the socialization process. If educators were to explain this to students instead of the usual "learn it because you'll need it sometime in the future," perhaps it would be met with less resistance.

Logical relationships are a result of one's ability to classify objects and ideas and to verbalize both the differences and the likenesses of objects, things, people, etc. Relationships are an integral part of higher reasoning in many areas. The ultimate goal is that of logical thought. The subskills include progressively matching identical elements, categorization of similar elements, and verbal classification and association. In this area also, there is a very large impact upon socialization.

The last of the conceptual skills is that of comprehension. This is defined as the ability to use judgment and reasoning in common sense situations. We usually simply state that an individual either does or does not have good common sense. One should have a common sense understanding of a situation, be able to follow directions and demonstrate insight, and, on a higher level, be able to comprehend abstracts. Remembering that the small infant believes that a person has disappeared when the hands cover the face and magically reappears to say, "Boo," we are reminded that the less sophisticated mind can only comprehend the concrete.

Social Skills

An area often overlooked in the development of the individual is that of proper social skills. These include social acceptance, anticipatory response, value judgment, and social maturity. A deficit in these areas can precipitate any problem in conceptual skills, language development, or perceptual motor skills.

One of the most important ideas that a young person can develop is that of peaceful coexistence with one's peers. Proper development includes acceptance in both a one-to-one relationship as well as group situations. Self-control, cooperation, and good manners are all teachable skills. The idea that these skills are innate and that some parents are *lucky* to have children with such skills does not take into account the learning process associated with such skills. Both home and school are responsible for their proper development. The three steps to complete social acceptance begin with self-acceptance, for one cannot begin to accept anything else if the self is not accepted. Family acceptance is the next step since the nuclear family plays such an important role in the development of the person. This is the reason that children who lack sufficient development in this step have such a difficult time with the third step, school and community acceptance. Unfortunately, many programs fail to include self-acceptance, which is actually the cornerstone for everything else.

An extension of logical skills, which was included in conceptual skills, is the social skill of anticipatory response. One should be able to anticipate the probable outcome of a social situation by logical inference. Being responsible for one's own actions is an exceedingly important learned social skill.

Value judgments certainly differ from one culture to another and we can only conclude that the individual must operate within the boundaries of his or her native culture. Everyone should have the ability to recognize and respond to moral and ethical issues. A young child needs to develop a proper sense of right and wrong. The process of continually adhering to consistent standards of right and wrong develops good value judgment. A proper program includes decisions regarding moral issues, patriotism, and ethical and rational behavior. Society's standards change from time to time, but certain judgments are universal.

Social maturity is more or less a catchall phrase that encompasses the previous three. While such terms as "mature, independent, and socially aware" are abstract. They emphasize the ideas of social maturity. Home and school should provide individuals with the opportunity to practice these skills by guided decision making. This is not to suggest that a young person be given complete open choices in certain areas. Rather the decision should be structured in such a manner as to make the more acceptable choice the path of least resistance. Much of personal success is based upon social maturity.

PSYCHOMETRIC TESTING

Math fright, or any other pseudonym that one prefers to use, is a common barrier in the effective use of statistics and psychometrics in today's psychology. That, in turn, directly hampers one of the most useful evaluative tools, the psychometric tests. While all the literature reviewed on statistics and psychometrics went into much process detail, though some were labelled elementary or basic, it appears that a need exists for a simple "Glossary of Statistical and Psychometric Terms." It is considerably doubtful that the vast majority of behavioral science experts are fluid with the complete computation of an ANOVA technique, nor should that be necessary. Certainly, a profession which prides itself on the ability to relate and communicate to people can find a better way to make the numbers game less threatening. "No pain, no gain" is an addage to be used in a gym or health spa, not in a professional curriculum. Lest the entire idea be analyzed at the stake by the more astute, allow it to be suggested that, as a scientific discipline, psychology does need to treat data in a sound statistical manner. It is merely being suggested that one should not require intense psychotherapy as a result of that exposure.

In consideration that *The Eight Mental Measurements Yearbook* (15) lists almost 1,200 tests, it would be impractical as well as useless to name all of them. There are, however, a number of instruments that are more frequently used by clinicians and can be understood by all involved in education. This certainly does not imply that any of the others are insignificant. In fact, many of the more specific tests allow one to pinpoint more specifically areas of strengths and weaknesses. A good example of this would be in the case of analyzing potential for suicide. The point to stress is that these assessment tools have many interpretations and one needs to obtain the whole picture of the individual or situations before drawing any conclusions from one scale of one test.

A person could easily spend hours pouring over the almost 1,200 tests, more when unpublished materials are considered. Those working with a learning disabled athlete need to familiarize themselves with psychometric instruments for two reasons. First, if the person has been extensively tested then much information can be gleaned from previous efforts. Second, if someone has not been tested, then by having a broad familiarity with instruments one might more easily recognize an existing problem and be able to refer to the proper source. Obviously, the following descriptions are intended only to list the tests for those familiar with them and to introduce them to those who are unfamiliar. Further information may be gathered from other sources. Many references simply list the test with a brief description of the structure and specific use. *Standards for Educational and Psychological Tests* (8) by the APA cites the responsibilities of both the test manufacturer and the test administrator. Psychological testing has come a long way since Binet's first intelligence test in 1905, but it still has a very long way to go before it can be considered even close to exact.

Tests are classified into standardized versus nonstandardized, the former being one of the most important contributions in terms of scientific data. The establishment of norms with the standardized test makes its use far more reliable. However, it should be noted that when working with the psychological aspects of an individual, the norm is not what is significant, but rather the intuition and insight of the tester. Keeping that premise in mind, many of the nonstandardized tests can be of great use. Tests are also classified as individual vs. group, speed vs. power, objective vs. nonobjective, and cognitive, including aptitude and achievement vs. affective.

In 1976 a survey by Brown and McGuire (2:12) examined the most frequently used clinical assessment instruments. In order, these were: Wechsler Intelligence Scale for Children (WISC); Bender Visual Motor Gestalt; Wechsler Adult Intelligence Scale (WAIS); Minnesota Multiphasic Personality Inventory (MMPI); Rorschach Inkblot Test; Thematic Apperception Test (TAT); Draw-a-Person Test (Goodenough); House-Tree-Person Technique (HTP); and Stanford-Binet Intelligence Test. In addition, a survey conducted showed that psychologists also suggested that clinical psychology students familiarize themselves with: Halstead-Reitan Neuropsychological Battery; Illinois Test of Psycholinguistic Abilities; Wide Range Achievement Tests; and the 16 Personality Factor Test (16PF). Accurately stated, it is evident that the clinician must be skilled in psychometric testing and evaluation. Each of the tests mentioned, as well as all others, have at least one complete manual for scoring and interpretation. Many of the more popular assessment tools have had numerous publications on just the interpretation aspect. The Rorschach is a good example of this. For this reason testing has become a specialty within the field of clinical psychology. Many clinicians refer out for testing and then draw conclusions and courses of action from the results.

More work has been done with achievement tests than in any other area. However, the basic rules of preparation are true for all areas of psychometrics. There are numerous considerations in test making such as length, format, method of recording answers, directions for the administration and testing conditions. All of these play a significant role in the use of the test. While most test making is left up to the professional test-making organizations, the clinician should at least be familiar with the components.

Norms, Reliability, and Validity

Whether it be age and grade norms, percentile norms, or standard score norms, all of the major tests have used some form of standardization. The important concept to understand is that the norms provide a reasonably accurate means of induction and interpretation. Those using the results of the tests are able to accurately diagnose and prescribe remediation and compensation knowing that test results have been proven in the past. Generally speaking, the more a test is researched and used the more accurate the norms. Yet, even with a test such as the MMPI, there is still much controversy as to the data relevant to current times since the norms were established decades ago in an almost rural population.

The reliability of the test refers to its relative freedom from unsystematic errors of measurement. The test must be consistent in what it measures. This is usually checked by test-retest, split-half, or Kuder-Richardson methods, all of which can be obtained from a statistics book if one is that interested. From a scientific data standpoint the reliability of a test is a very important function.

The traditional definition of test validity is the extent to which a test measures what it purports to measure. These include content validity, concurrent validity, predictive validity, criterion-related validity, and construct validity.

Achievement Tests

These are by far the most popular types of tests. The achievement tests measure the level of knowledge, skill, and accomplishment in a particular area of endeavor. These are tests that are direct measures of what they are designed to measure. The four general types of achievement tests are survey test batteries, survey tests in specific subjects, diagnostic tests, and prognostic tests.

The Comprehensive Test of Basic Skills (CTBS), Wide Range Achievement Tests (WRAT), and the Peabody Individual Achievement Tests (PIAT) are designed to measure broad areas of reading, language, math, reference skills, science, and social studies. They are divided into levels of skills. Large school districts, such as the Los Angeles Unified School District, use such tests. Other general tests in this area include the Iowa Test of Basic Skills, Metropolitan Achievement Tests, Sequential Test of Educational Progress (STEP), SRA Achievement Series, and Stanford Achievement Tests. There are also tests such as the Tests of Adult Basic Education (TABE) and Fundamental Achievement Series that are designed to measure basic skills in adults having less than a high school education.

Because many of the problems associated with school are related to problems in reading, many tests have been designed to assess this skill. Buros (15) even has a separate book compiled on reading tests. Oftentimes this area is the presenting problem with the student encumbered by a learning disability. Survey reading tests measure a person's overall abilities. They usually include sections of vocabulary and comprehension. Two of the most prominent are the Gates-MacGinitie Reading Test and the Nelson Reading Test.

The most common type of diagnostic test is the diagnostic reading test. They attempt to assess many different factors affecting reading, such as intelligence, motivation, eye-hand coordination, perceptual ability, and the ability to understand concepts. Examples are Diagnostic Reading Scales (DRS); Gates-McKillop Reading Diagnostic Test, and Stanford Diagnostic Reading Test. The assessment and interpretation from these tests are invaluable when recognizing and working with the learning disabled athlete because of the broad picture that the results can present.

Often used for placement is the reading readiness test. This measures the extent to which a child possesses the skills and knowledge for learning to read. They usually contain visual discrimination, auditory blending and discrimination, vocabulary, symbol recognition, and visual motor coordination. Two prominent tests in this area are Gates-MacGinitie Readiness Skills Test and Metropolitan Readiness Tests. Often times many of the disabilities can be diagnosed at an early age with the use of one of these instruments.

Mathematics tests are also classified as survey, diagnostic, and prognostic. The survey tests are designed to encompass both the knowledge and application of various mathematical skills. The Cooperative Mathematics Tests and the Stanford Mathematics Test are representative of the survey tests in this area. Perhaps the most widely used of the diagnostic mathematics tests is the Stanford Diagnostic Mathematics Test. Tests such as this attempt to assess a more complex subject involving a great variety of skills. It should be remembered that mathematics abilities affect much more than simply the juggling of numbers in one's mind. Conceptualization is often affected by mathematics abilities. Prognostic tests in math are not widely used. Usually the only areas to be tested are algebra and geometry.

Language tests are primarily verbal, but measures of nonverbal communication, even with normal people, are also being used. A test such as the Boehm Test of Basic Concepts can determine a child's understanding of fifty basic concepts of space, quantity, and time necessary to master language. Specifically in English, tests such as the Cooperative English Tests and Brown-Carlsen Listening Comprehension Test measure a variety of skills including reading comprehension level, vocabulary, speed of comprehension, English expression, and the spoken language.

Additional achievement tests are in the areas of foreign language (MLA—Cooperative Foreign Language Tests and Modern Language Aptitude Tests), social studies (Cooperative Social Studies Tests), professions (GRE, LSAT, NTE, and MCAT), and business and skilled trades. They provide a more specific view of technical aspects of skills.

Intelligence Tests

Two tests of intelligence are more commonly used than all others. They are the Stanford-Binet and the Wechsler Series (WISC-R, WAIS-R, and WPPSI). The former was responsible for the "IQ" concept, but the latter has many more clinical applications since it reveals scaled subtest scores and three deviation IQ's—verbal, performance and full scale. These can reveal organic brain damage and certain mental disorders. It should be noted by the person working with the learning disabled athlete that the Wechsler series is usually the test of choice when assessing learning disabilities because of its ability to pinpoint problems. The WAIS-R has twelve subtests: information; picture completion; digit span; picture arrangement; vocabulary; block design; arithmetic; object assembly; comprehension; digit symbol; similarities; and level aspiration. The correlation of the WAIS-R and the Stanford-Binet is about .85 with the S-B being higher at the high and lower at the low end because of the difference in standard deviation. A trick of the educational trade is to use the Stanford-Binet when the Wechsler has shown individuals to be at either end of the spectrum. This would ensure that those people qualify for programs at either the higher end, gifted, or lower end, basic, as the case may dictate.

Golden gives an excellent clinical interpretation of the WAIS (39:13) and goes on further to explain the Performance IQ-Verbal IQ Difference (39:28). He does cite studies to show how brain damage and psychiatric disorders can be diagnostically observed. One important point stressed is that of individual observation in addition to straight statistical analysis. Perhaps the most comprehensive research involving the WAIS as it relates to psychological assessment and neurological functioning was conducted by Reitan in 1966 (2:144). As an example, a Verbal IQ significantly lower than a Performance IQ is a diagnostic sign of left hemisphere damage; a lower than VIQ is a sign of right hemisphere damage.

Many times the WAIS is used in conjunction with the Bender Visual Motor Gestalt to more specifically assess the problem. The Wide-Range Achievement Test (WRAT) has also proved useful in the assessment of learning disabilities.

Other intelligence tests that are useful when time and reading skills are limited include the Peabody Picture Vocabulary Test-Revised (PPVT-R), Columbia Mental Maturity Scale (CMMS), Ammons Full Range Picture Vocabulary Test, Shipley-Hartford Scale, Raven's Progressive Matrices, and the Leiter International Performance Scale.

There are even tests to measure the intelligence of infants and the very young. Two such tests are a downward extension of the Stanford-Binet and the Bagley Scales of Infant Development. Unfortunately, some parents use these to salve their own egos by comparing their own newborn to another. These were not the purposes for which the tests were designed.

There have been many suggestions that IQ tests are subject to cultural awareness. The Culture Fair Intelligence Test is an attempt to limit bias from intelligence assessment. Even such tests as the Dove and the Bitch-100 (Black Intelligence Test of Cultural Homogeneity) have been devised to counter balance some of the standard tests.

A tremendous amount of research has gone and is going on to determine which factors have an effect on intelligence. These include heredity, environment, brain structure, hormones, drugs, climate, and nutrition. There still are no definitive answers.

Special Abilities

Many times tests of special abilities are labelled "aptitude" tests. They are a measurement primarily of potential achievement or to predict a level of future performance. Many of these tests are performance-oriented rather than a mere pencil and paper type of test. Remembering that the normal intelligence test measures approximately 8 of the more than 100 identified types of intelligence, these types of tests give a much broader picture of the individual.

Sensory tests fall under this classification. The Snellen eye chart is a measure of visual acuity. An audiometer producing an audiogram is a measure of auditory acuity. The Ishihara Test for Color Blindness and the Dvorine Color Vision Test are also tests of special abilities. These serve to assess one specific function. If a more comprehensive examination is required, then visual screening instruments, such as the B & L Vision Tester, are used.

The Frostig Developmental Test of Visual Perception (DTVP) is a good example of a sensorimotor test battery. It measures eye-motor coordination, figure-ground, constancy of shape, position in space, and spatial relationships.

Tests of psychomotor skills were among the first measures of special abilities to be designed. Fleischman (2:208) identified eleven psychomotor factors: aim; arm-hand steadiness; control precision; finger dexterity; manual dexterity; multilimb coordination; rate control; reaction time; response orientation; speed of arm movement; and wrist-finger speed. Large manual movements can be assessed by the Stromberg Dexterity Test or the Minnesota Rate of Manipulation Test. Small manual movements are tested by the O'Connor Finger Dexterity Test, O'Connor Tweezer Dexterity Test, Purdue Pegboard, and the Crawford Small Parts Dexterity Test. Many of the aforementioned skills are important in the athletic arena. Unknown to many working in sport, numerous areas of giftedness can be accurately tested and measured.

Other special ability test areas include spatial relations (Minnesota Spatial Relations Test), mechanical ability (MacQuarrie Test for Mechanical Ability, Bennett Mechanical Comprehension Test), clerical (Minnesota Clerical Test), computers (Computer Programmer Aptitude Battery, Computer Operator Aptitude Battery), art (Meir Art Tests, Graves Design Judgment Test, Horn Art Aptitude Inventory), and music (Seashore Measures of Musical Talents, Wing Standardized Tests of Musical Intelligence, Musical Aptitude Profile).

Aptitude tests have also been developed and standardized as predictors of academic achievement. Examples in this area are the Primary Mental Abilities Tests (PMA), the Guilford-Zimmerman Aptitude Survey, and the Differential Aptitude Tests (DAT). Reliability coefficients are high, and these tests have been shown to be good predictors of high school and college grades.

General aptitude tests have gained much attention since the Army stated using them in World War II. At the same time, the Army used the tests as a means of classifying men into skilled and unskilled jobs and to determine who would profit from further training.

In summary, almost every area in which some type of skill is involved can be tested. It is important to use a test that has been standardized so that its reliability will remain high.

Interest, Attitude, and Values

Affective test instruments are typically not as objective as cognitive tests. There are those professionals who suggest that these are not tests at all. Nonetheless, they offer the clinician good insight into the "inner" person. It should be noted, however, that a complete evaluation of the individual should not be based on the results of one of these instruments.

Both the Strong-Campbell Interest Inventory and the Kuder Preference Record and Interest-Surveys are designed to examine an individual's likes and dislikes. They are useful in guiding a person in the selection of occupations and hobbies. For special situations there are also inventories for children and the disadvantaged.

Attitudes are learned. By drawing upon prior experiences the individual can respond positively or negatively to many things. This differs from opinions which are very specific to one given situation. The attitude is developed over a long period of time whereas the opinion may change rapidly. They are useful clinically in a number of ways. Commercial polls determine attitudes of segments of the population, while individual attitude insight gives the clinician further information with which to work.

Value is the importance or worth that an individual places on particular activities or objects. Rokeach's Value Survey has been used extensively in comparative and cross-cultural research. The Survey of Interpersonal Values and the Survey of Personal Values, both by Gorden, give an excellent profile of what the examinee holds dear. This can be reassessed after therapy to determine changes.

Personality

Even though there are a myriad of psychometric tools for the assessment of personality, three fall into the top six of all clinical assessment instruments (as listed previously). These are the Rorschach Inkblot, the Thematic Apperception Test, and the Minnesota Multiphasic Personality Inventory. The first two are projective tests in that they allow the clinician to assess possible future actions, while the MMPI is a criterion-keyed inventory. Also noteworthy, though far less used, is the 16 Personality Factor Questionnaire. The 16PF was designed for working with normal people and, therefore, does not focus on pathological traits as does the MMPI.

The Rorschach and TAT are whole studies unto themselves. Each has no less than five books written on interpretation, and then each has parented further projective techniques. It appears that more clinicians are beginning to use the TAT, now, because it is a less subjective instrument. This would be consistent with the current trend to produce results more closely modeled to true scientific form.

The validity of the MMPI two-point code has been questioned. But it has stood the test of the academicians and naysayers for a long time. It is a highly useful starting point in the interpretation of scores.

Neuropsychological Tests

Though such tests as the Bender and the Benton have already been mentioned, it should be pointed out that more research is being produced in this area that is of extreme importance to the clinician. Neuropsychological testing represents a major segment of assessment done by psychologists. Concerning the learning disabled athlete, results from these tests shed immense light on the reasons for, and therefore subsequent remediation of, at least coping strategies for a variety of situations.

As an aid, neuropsychological tests can be used to confirm a neuro-diagnosis. This can be related to a functional disorder or bring into focus additional problems concerning the origin of a particular disability. These tests are also useful tools in establishing a baseline and subsequent improvement or decline. Results of the tests may also be used for their prognostic value and are an aid in planning rehabilitation programs.

Two of the most comprehensive of these are the Halstead-Reitan Neuropsychological Battery and the Luria-Nebraska Neuropsychological Battery. Either may be used to point out cerebrovascular disorders, multiple sclerosis, presenile dementia, Parkinson's disease, tumors, and other problems used in conjunction with a test such as the WAIS-R, they represent a much more complete picture of the individual.

Suicide

"Suicide is the only mental health problem that has death as a very real end (60:124)." As such it can almost be evaluated by itself. With the number of teenage suicides rising to epidemic proportions, the diagnosis for the potential for suicide has begun to come into sharp focus. Several assessment tools have been devised such as the Beck Scales, the Scale of Suicide Intent by Pierce (1977), the Index of Potential Suicide by Zung (1974), the Suicide Death Prediction Scale by Lettieri (1974), and the

Risk-Rescues Rating by Weisman and Worden (1974). The major difficulty with these instruments is the lack of norms and standardization. This may be due in part to the recency of their development. They certainly offer a useful projective tool. Considering the high stressful atmosphere surrounding athletics, a good working knowledge of aspects of suicide is important. The frustrations of the athlete are only compounded by a learning disability that may take someone to the brink of disaster. Still to be evaluated is the athlete who commits suicide in the figurative sense as opposed to the literal sense.

Practical Application

Through the review of literature it has become apparent that psychometric evaluations have not been accorded the proper place in the assessment of the individual. While certainly not suggesting using them exclusively, many psychologists acknowledge a lack of use due to a lack of expertise in interpretation. Utilized to its fullest potential, a valid assessment tool used in conjunction with other tests and techniques offers much in background information, providing a basis for diagnosis and prognosis. Oftentimes this can be accomplished with a great reduction of time, a precious commodity when dealing with an athlete.

The ethics of psychological testing, as defined by the American Psychological Association, are quite specific. The responsibility for quality tools falls on the test manufacturer as well as on the person administering the test. Allowing any part of a test to carelessly come into public view invalidates the instrument. Furthermore, only those specified as qualified to administer and those deemed qualified to interpret should be allowed to perform those respective functions. If these standards are not upheld, a valuable psychological tool becomes misused and useless. Confidentiality must be maintained both with the test, itself, as well as with the results and interpretations.

The administration of the tests, while certainly ensuring reliability, is only the beginning. Interpretation, prognosis, and prescriptive action require the highest degree of professional expertise. Many of the instruments, such as the Rorschach and the TAT, do not have objective interpretations. Symptoms of psychopathology or other malfunctions may be present, but it takes a highly skilled clinician to assess a difficulty and prescribe treatment. It is important that those dealing with the athlete limit themselves to their own areas of expertise.

The positive aspects of psychological assessment are significant. Used properly, they are a valuable tool with which to aid others. The psychological profession has attempted to maintain high standards so that there may be a high level of confidence in the available tests. The person dealing with the learning disabled athlete should make full use of the results gathered from the administration of these instruments. Again, the same diagnosed problems that affect the academic performance hamper the individual's athletic performance.

The negative aspects are twofold. Many times there are those who use the results for the basis of all future actions. Too often these tests are misused either by incorrect administration or by a quasi professional interpretation, though this is not in compliance with the APA guidelines. As such, the very foundation for treatment is set up for no results at best and actual psychological damage at the worst. Secondly, too often psychologists place an over-inflated emphasis on the results of one test, resulting in a skewed view. The literature continually reiterated that an assessment instrument is only part of the overall picture and that observation and questioning, more appropriately termed empathetic listening, hold a greater position. Much of the public's negative feelings toward the profession stem from the misuse of psychometrics.

SOCIALIZATON IN ATHLETICS

Though the idea of social psychology has been present almost since psychology itself, recency has seen an incredible surge in the quantity of writing. Neal even suggests that, "Social psychology is a legitimate child of the twentieth century (63:3)." Today we recognize that social life is always in the process of change and development. Relationships are ever-changing as people move in and out of the lives of others. Prior psychologies dealt more with the isolated person, and the recent focus has illuminated the idea that the self rests within the larger circle of society. What we see and do in the world, as well as within ourselves, is shaped by the interactions with the many people in our lives. The theories of object relations stress this premise. Psychological libraries have more and more recent publications in this area than in any other. That social psychology has established a premier position is a point that cannot be contested.

Entering into this emerging area comes the field of sports psychology. Athletics is an intensified microcosm of social psychology, yet with many of its own rules, regulations, and, of course, problems. While social psychology alone deals with the individual and her or his interactions with the group, the social psychology of athletics deals with a triad—the individual, the team, and the crowd. Whether sport should hold the position in our society that it does is probably debatable. That it, in fact, does hold a revered position is not a contestable point. No other aspect of society other than business, has an entire section of every major newspaper dedicated to it. No other events stir the emotions like the traditional rivalries that occur on all levels of sport. Even for the crowds, the socialization process occurring during athletic events is quantitatively more, and is far more intense, than the average person is exposed to.

In dealing with athletics one needs to examine all the various aspects of the social psychology. The advocates of sport have for years suggested that the positive aspects of comradery, common goals, and team identity are carried over into everyday life. In their endeavors to promote their ideas, they, of course, have failed to mention that the negative aspects, such as substance abuse, a win-at-all-costs ethic, and the dehumanizing effects, are also often carried over. One needs to consider the components of the triad, their interactions, and both the positive and negative effects. The stress of the athletic arena, itself, has created innumerable disorders that most often have gone unrecognized.

Role of the Athlete

The role of the athlete is often paradoxical. As an example, it is often said that a particular individual must have had "incredible self-discipline to reach the level that he or she has reached." That would assume that the person is very capable of controlling all the various factors necessary to achieve optimum performance. Yet, at that same moment that athlete has a curfew, diet restrictions, rules of conformity, in essence a rigidly structured life style. And this is even true on the professional level with mature men and women in their thirties and forties. So, what then is really being observed?

To begin with, the athletic roots of the inividual need to be thoroughly examined. The possibilities are numerous and maybe any one or a combination of a number of factors. Superior coordination certainly plays an integral role. But so often there appears the individual who, with only average athletic abilities, did it all by the proverbial "hard work and effort." Parental pressure may explain much about the drive of the athlete. Athletics may have been the sole source of positive reinforcement for that particular individual. The mental mechanism of identification, hero worship, may have had a significant influence. Peer pressure may have necessitated directing pursuits in a particular direction. And so the beginnings are often full of complexities, but they all result in a specific social role definition.

A significant portion of the athlete's self-worth comes from the other two parts of the triad. The team and the crowd play a very important part in the developmental aspect of the athlete. At an early age superior performance is applauded repeatedly and rewarded with medals, trophies, plaques, and ribbons. Unfortunately, poor performance is often booed, even with younger children, with a resulting withdrawal from competitive situations and possible stress complications. As Hunt states, "Most psychologists agree that the identity of any human being is a consequence of the interaction between the genetic material with which an individual is provided at conception and the myriad events in that individual's life (45:19)." Returning to the initial member of the triad, the social role of the athlete is examined.

While the athletic community is certainly as diverse as the general population, if not more so, certain characteristics are present even with the various sports. A certain decorum presents in the sports world. Perhaps the infatuation with sport stems from the early Greeks and before. But one thing is certain. The whole world, even the world of academia, appreciates a superior athletic performance. The lives of the top athletes are closely monitored, and they often become national heroes, exemplified by Babe Ruth, Joe Di Maggio, Pelé, Nadia Comanici, and Olga Korbut, Chris Everett Lloyd, to name only a few. Muhammed Ali became somewhat of an unofficial ambassador for the United States as a result of his career. To reach that level an individual must have drive, which includes self-discipline, determination, and confidence. He or she must be willing to sacrifice time, energy, and, in many cases, money to achieve superior performance. But most cannot travel the road to success alone. For each person that makes it at any level there will have been a consistent support network. To really reach the top an individual needs to be driven beyond what they may view as limits of physical pain, but more importantly psychological pain. They must be able to focus in on a singular goal with no distractions. Sports psychologist, Dr. Robert Nideffer, concludes that an athlete's problem, regardless of what sport, is to maintain arousal, the peak at which skills are sharpest, without slipping over the edge into loss of concentration or pressing too hard. For many athletes this becomes a source of conflict. Babad, Birnbaum, and Benne (11:49) call selective attention a detrimental quality that is an obstacle to self-awareness. Yet this is precisely what the athlete needs to accomplish, a blocking of most of the stimuli surrounding him or her. But this should only be done during the moment of training and competition. How easily stated in an academic paper. In reality, those athletes in control learn to *throw the switch,* to concentrate and then turn it off to socialize. The socially unskilled athlete, no matter how superior in motor skills, begins to react the same off court as on court, John McEnroe personified over and over again. Mr. McEnroe is certainly not alone in this characteristic. But the real question is, "Can *any* athlete truly turn the switch completely?

One must understand that the reason most athletes have trouble relinquishing the spotlight is because of a deep fear. For years self-worth came from fine accomplishments. Many look at videos, pictures, and movies and reach the conclusion that they are, in fact, as good as people have been telling them. When all this positive reinforcement is suddenly withdrawn, the result is oftentimes socially and psychologically disastrous. The athlete must reevaluate and find another social role. The ensuing confusion often leads down a road that ends in something less than a socially desirable role.

Not everyone with superior athletic skills is capable of becoming a star. It takes far more than most people realize to achieve the level of success that most only read about on the front page of the sports section or on the cover of Sports Illustrated.

The sports psychologist needs to assume the role of a personality adviser. It would be of infinite value to an athlete to carefully examine his or her role in the complete picture and to determine in what direction events are headed. The learning disabled athlete is even in greater need since the end of an athletic career often leaves virtually nothing. The purpose would be twofold. First, the individual would feel more in control and, second, the continuous transition from lay person to athlete and back would result in the athlete's bottom line, better performance.

The Social Psychology of a Team

Certainly the collective personalities of the players is an integral part of the team personality. But there should be little doubt that a good portion of this team personality stems from the coach. His particular style, her emphasis, his disciplinary tactics, her sense of humor all play prominent roles in the molding of the team as a unit. The Los Angeles Raiders are known as aggressive renegades much as a result of managing partner Al Davis and the hands off, laissez-faire attitude of Tom Flores as coach. Former Raider coach John Madden had many practical jokers on his team as a result of his own escapades.

There are those who are leaders and those who are followers, those who motivate and those who need motivation, those whose sole interest is in themselves and those who sacrifice for the good of the whole team. Here, once again, arises a very fine line between maximum team effort and total loss of self-identity. The athlete actually goes through each process of social psychology twice, once on an individual basis and once on a team identity basis. Self-inquiry must take place in both individual and team psyches for the end result of a cohesive performance to be successful. One specific area that needs to be addressed is an establishing and pursuing of a team social identity. By working through various strategies the groundwork can be laid for the team to function in an autonomous fashion.

The normal pathologies that are present in society are also present on a team and very often magnified because of pressure. Such factors as prejudice in race, ethnicity, religion, sex roles, and age are all problems that, left untouched, can greatly undermine the goals of the team. For the learning disabled athlete the problem that caused him or her to retreat prior to athletics can once again act to the detriment of the individual if those in charge are not cognizant of team social psychology.

As Cohen suggests, we are literally "constructing" a structure. We need to have a very solid base and we need to repair or replace any defective materials (22:195). Each piece needs to be worked on, polished, and then integrated into the whole. An outstanding team is actually greater than the sum of its parts.

As Michael Magoney, clinical psychologist at Pennsylvania State University states, "The difference between two athletes is 20 percent physical and 80 percent mental." The team needs to provide the environment for the individual to flourish and grow. That growing individual then has an obligation to add to that extra dimension of esprit de corps. One does not function successfully without the other.

Anger and Aggression

One of the particular oddities that the athlete is involved in is the phenomena of anger and aggression. Harari and Kaplan remark that,

"Throughout recorded history aggressive behavior has remained one of the most intriguing mysteries of human behavior (43:155)." Paradoxically, almost all human societies have condemned aggression and fighting but have made heroes of individuals who were brutally aggressive in appropriate areas, sublimation at its ultimate. The field of athletic competition is one such area. To punch someone into oblivion is considered the art of a great boxer and is handsomely rewarded. To thrust a powerful forearm across someone's face is the sign of a good defensive lineman. To deliver a blow with one's shoulders and head powerful enough to dislocate limbs is the trademark of an elite defensive back. So much is violence a part of hockey that a player was recently benched for refusing to participate in a team brawl against another team. Many an athlete has been urged to go out there and "kill your opponent." Consider much of the common phraseology of football: the bomb, blitz, cut block, neutral zone, blast, trap, rip block, clothesline, intercept. These all carry the connotation of the game itself.

The problem is that most who urge this reckless abandon of sanity are not aware that with a loss of control comes a loss of concentration. There are bound to be situations that make athletes mad regardless of the sport. Aggressiveness is a desirable characteristic of athletes in all sports. However, this should be controlled and channelled into constructive action. An athlete needs to create a psychological game plan, as well as a physical game plan, to deal with all possibilities.

Since aggression is labelled a masculine trait, and yet important for the female competitor, the mixed message often creates deep psychological problems. This is further compounded by the label of "tomboy" that some still ascribe to female competitors. Female athletes have made great strides in breaking that stereotype. Yet the chosen sports (by whom is an interesting question) of female competition are considered safe in that not a great deal of anger and aggression is outward. Take for example gymanstics, swimming, volleyball, tennis, etc. Not until recently have women body builders entered into competition, along with women weight lifters. But the governing body in female body building has not arrived at a decision as to how the female body should look. The message is that females can get a bit flustered and upset, but they should not get mad, angry, or aggressive because it is not lady-like. But at the same time, as long as they are at it, everyone demands a top-notch performance.

Psychological Training and the Psych Game

Sometimes it is simply not enough to go out and do your best. Since it has already been stated that sport is 10 to 20 percent physical and 80 to 90 percent psychological one must often attempt to knock an opponent off her or his path of concentration. This can be accomplished in a number of ways, but basically with an increased understanding of social psychology the individual can better determine which approach to use.

It is not uncommon for players on the professional level to be given an entire docier on an opponent, including habits, friends, and family. The purpose is to gain a thorough understanding of precisely what are motivational factors of the opponent and to be able to make an educated guess as to the opponent's mindset prior to competition. In this way each player becomes mentally prepared to deal with an opponent. Not only must today's athletes be masters of themselves, but must be masters of their opponents as well.

The Psych game has no limits in sports. The creativity of the individual is free to roam. Anything from a furrowed brow look to wild and outrageous antics are a part of the game. Though no other field of psychology may wish to claim it, the Psych game rightfully belongs in social psychology. It is, after all, an exercise in dealng with others in the context of a social setting (no matter how distorted that may appear). The following case history should explain precisely what this game is all about.

NATE: Several years ago one of the authors had a wide receiver on his football team, by the name of Nate. Nate was a fine receiver, blessed with excellent speed and very good leaping ability. Halfway through the season he was ranked as the second leading receiver among the local high schools. Prior to a game, one of the opponents brought out an individual dressed in what appeared to be one of Nate's team's jerseys. He kept falling down, missing the ball, and stumbling. During the first several minutes of the game, three members of the opposing team legally cracked Nate no matter where he was on the field. This occurred for no longer than the first five minutes of the game. It only needed to be that long. Even though they never touched him again, nor even talked to him, Nate did not catch one ball the entire game. In fact, he dropped three touchdown passes with no one around him. So effective had their psychological ploy been that the reason there was no one around him was that they gambled and only covered him 50 percent of the time. They had obviously done their homework and found that Nate was easily excitable and quickly provoked into being out of control.

Nate, not being one to pass up a learning experience, took notes. During a subsequent play-off game with another team, he quietly began talking to the player assigned to cover him. According to Nate, and verified by his teammates, he mentioned that the other young man was not blessed with particularly good facial features, that his mother was remiss in not providing him with better attire, and that this other young man had a proclivity for engaging in incestuous impulses with his maternal progenitor. As a result, Nate set a school record for most passes caught in one game and was on the receiving end of a pass play that set a record as the longest play in the history of the school, 98 yards.

Incidents such as these are not at all uncommon in sport. Quite the contrary, they are becoming a greater part of the psychological preparation of teams. Critics contend that all this has nothing to do with athletic performance. That is certainly a debatable topic. But not debatable is the responsibility to prepare individuals for these possibilities. Referring back to Dr. Nideffer's comment that focus on purpose is paramount, one can readily observe that psychological training plays a significant role. From the perspective of one working with a learning handicapped person, the more adequately prepared an athlete can be made, the easier it is to overcome and compensate for liabilities.

Crowds — The Productive and Detrimental Aspects

Completing the unique triad in sport is the crowd. The athletes would not exist without them, and yet the crowd is often the direct cause of stress and early retirement, the paradoxical "can't live with them and can't live without them." There obviously is no way for the athlete to control the crowd. So it is paramount that steps be taken to control the one aspect of the event that is left, him or herself.

As a segment of social psychology, the mood of a crowd sways with the momentum of the game. No one involved in athletics would dare deny the positive influences of the proverbial home court advantage. The crowd provides a number of positive influences on the athletic performance of the team as a whole and the individuals which include both physical and psychological elements. First, everyone loves recognition, and while adulation from one's peers provides certain comforts, the acclamation by 50-100,000 spectators is a big fulfillment of a ravenous ego. As in the simplest psychological experiments, positive reinforcement provides the basis for a continued behavior. Much has been done in the professional arenas to bring forth the best in the crowd, though precisely what that is may be arguable. The organ playing "charge," the

Dallas Cowgirls, the San Diego Chicken, mascots, cheerleaders, and yell leaders are all designed to rally support of the crowd behind the team. While it is fun, its intent is serious business, which on most levels translates into money. The realist is aware that the successful performance of a team will result in the crowd financially contributing to future endeavors.

And the crowd does not go away without certain psychological benefits as well. Most noteworthy is the cathartic effect that a good team performance has on the crowd. The team also provides many with a great sense of identity, as evidenced by the enormous alumni associations of schools like USC and UCLA. Traveling to other cities, one often crosses paths with a staunch supporter of another professional or college level team. The normal reaction is to defend one's hometown team, even if not particularly interested in that team while at home. So much so is the process of identification prevalent that many who were never even involved in a sport refer to "we" when relating stories about performances past, present, and future.

Unfortunately, there are also detrimental effects that manifest themselves mostly in individuals. The old addage, "Everyone likes a winner," is reasonably accurate. However, the additional phrase "And no one likes a loser," should be added. The feeling of rejection by a crowd can be horrendous, and, being a mob, they are often merciless and unrelenting. Pat Haden, former Rams quarterback, after being seriously injured heard the crowd cheer for his injury. He was incensed to the point that he remarked, "This is a game! What kind of animal cheers at the injury of a player? The purchase of a ticket does not entitle the bearer to act like an animal!" Yet, this is often an occurrence at various athletic events. The crowd also drives the players and coaches to a win-at-all-costs approach, whether it is by yelling and cheering or booing, as the case may be, or in an indirect approach, buying less tickets. This pressure translates into such actions as drug abuse, anxiety attacks, burn-out, and extending beyond limits with the result being serious injury.

The triad now being complete, one role of those working with the athlete becomes more evident. Elements must be balanced so that the result is a cohesive performance. While the crowd cannot be controlled, its effect upon the team and the individual can be structured in such a manner as to make the best use of the productive elements and to lessen the impact of the detrimental effects.

Again, stressing that athletics, even the individual sports, are very much social events, a tenet of social psychology can well be applied.

Whether right or wrong, men and women can no longer merely go out and "just play the game and have a good time." This reality should define the role of the clinician to assist individuals in making the best possible use of their talents.

Working on the individual level as blocks in the foundation leads to firm team structure. When those two fall into their proper places, the third element, the crowd, has a natural niche in which to fit. It is from this perspective that one can impact the social interaction of sport.

Chapter Three

SPECIFIC DISABILITIES MANIFEST
IN ATHLETICS

FROM empirical observation, compiled over a fifteen-year period, it appears that the percentage of those with learning disabilities, however marginal they may be, is greater in the athletic population than in the general population. Most assuredly before any conclusive evidence can be discussed or any figures extrapolated, a definitive study in that area needs to be undertaken. For obvious reasons the area of learning disabilities labelled gross motor development is rarely affected in a negative fashion. On the contrary, it generally appears to have been over-developed to compensate for a deficit in another area. Therapists working with the learning handicapped athlete will find that the means by which a person has compensated for a disability is oftentimes where this individual gets the proverbial *good strokes*.

In the area of sensorimotor integration the athlete appears smooth and fluid. But upon closer examination the observing therapist will be able to determine why certain sports were chosen. The spectrum is vast, ranging from the complexities of a sport, such as basketball or ice hockey, to an endurance activity, such as distance running. Sometimes coaches and parents attempt to force individuals into an appropriate activity where a skill deficit is not merely a lack of training and knowledge but rather a true disability. This is an area where thorough investigation prior to engaging in long practice hours should occur.

But what about the person who has the natural skills but appears uncoachable? What about the beautiful figure of grace that cannot remember her routine because, "You haven't studied hard enough and aren't dedicated enough"? For the first time, and it is long overdue, those involved in sports need to be concerned with and identify the learning disabled athlete. There are several major areas as they relate to sport.

Examples will be given in the major sports of football, basketball, and baseball, but similar problems may be modified in all other sports.

DISCUSSION OF PROBLEMS

If an athlete is told to do something and repeatedly does not perform the task, or performs something other than directed, an evaluation of auditory skills is in order. Each of these areas can be examined by simply recalling where the error took place and recreating the same situation. First, the athlete may have a loss in auditory acuity. The reasons may vary from fluid in the middle ear to a neurological impairment. The person working with the athlete would notice certain evaluative clues in particular situations. The following are examples of auditory acuity difficulties related to sports. Football: (1) On a number of occasions a player is called from the bench by the coach with no response, and other players, being the same distance away, must get the player's attention. (2) A player is continually called for late hits and claims he never heard a whistle. (3) A defensive back does not turn around to react to the football when teammates have yelled "Ball." (4) An offensive player continually asks the quarterback to repeat the signals in the huddle. Basketball: (1) A player continually does not respond to a coach's directions from the bench. (2) A player does not respond to teammates' verbal playmaking messages. (3) A player does not heed quiet, informal warnings by an official. Baseball: (1) An outfielder may not appear to move at the "crack of the bat." (2) A player is picked off at second base and appears not to have heard either the second baseman or shortstop coming in for the catch. (3) A runner does not hear commands from base coaches.

A disability in auditory decoding is somewhat more difficult to detect. The appearance of the problem results in a syndrome that may best be described by a lack of attention. The sounds are being heard, but the athlete does not indicate by gesture or words that the meaning of the auditory stimuli was understood. There is little or no differentiation from one sport to another. The athlete will look directly at the source of the stimulus. It will be obvious to the trained observer that the stimulus has been received, such as the action of visual contact. Yet either no action or incorrect action will result. Sometimes by persistence the athlete may perform correctly a percentage of the time. But the correct pattern will appear in a random fashion.

Auditory-vocal association problems may present themselves as a person who hears what was said, is further able to acknowledge the stimuli in a correct fashion, and yet proceeds to perform an incorrect or inappropriate action. Auditory-vocal association problems are differentiated from auditory decoding problems by observing that the athlete does not appear confused and appears to have fully understood. Football: (1) Upon hearing the signal for an interception, a defensive back stops, turns, and begins to tackle opposing players rather than block. (2) Upon hearing the signal for an intercepted ball, an offensive lineman stops, turns, and begins to block the opposition as opposed to tackling the ball carrier. (3) After hearing an opponent call for a fair catch on a punt, the player pauses for a moment and then tackles the opponent anyway. Basketball: (1) After hearing the playmaker give the number for a play, the player holds up the appropriate number of fingers to acknowledge receiving the stimulus, but he then executes the wrong play. (2) Upon being called for a fifth personal foul, a player holds his or her hand up as a sign of acknowledgment, but does not leave the court. Baseball: (1) A base runner nods at the base coach and then proceeds to perform the exact opposite of what was said. (2) A pitcher listens to a catcher's recommendations on a subsequent batter but then throws a wrong pitch, resulting in a devastating hit.

An auditory memory deficit is difficult in sport to differentiate from an auditory-vocal association. Both result in the same problem for the athlete, the resulting action is incorrect. The distinguishing characteristic would be that the auditory memory deficit would tend to have a greater time span. Whereas the auditory-vocal association is a difficulty with an immediate response, the auditory memory deficit would encompass things that have been explained previously. However, this may be relatively short. Football: (1) A player cannot remember what to do when the quarterback calls a particular play (longer time span). (2) A player designated as a messenger cannot remember the complete play as he runs it into the huddle (shorter time span). (3) A defensive player cannot remember specific down and distance instructions given to him by the coach immediately prior to the game. Basketball: (1) A player does not remember who to cover in different man-to-man defensive situations that were explained prior to the game. (2) A player cannot recall particular adjustment patterns made by the coach at halftime. (3) A player does not recall what was said to him during the game upon questioning the strategy the subsequent day. Baseball: (1) A player does not remember batting signals from the third base coach. (2) An outfielder has difficulty remembering who the relay man is in particular situations. (3) A catcher forgets the scouting report on batters.

An auditory sequencing problem would actually be observed as a continuing auditory memory deficit. The operative factor here is the inability to recall a series of auditory stimuli. So much of sport skills is a sequencing factor wherein difficulty causes much disarray. To be able to perform simple skills upon command would indicate an intact auditory memory, but the inability to put a sequence of skills together is an auditory sequencing problem. Football: (1) An offensive lineman can execute step, turn, run with a low center of gravity, and block inside out commands upon hearing the verbal cue. However, he cannot put these in the proper sequence upon hearing the encompassing term "trap block." (2) A receiver can do the proper footwork when hearing the commands to drive three steps out, then three steps in, followed by three steps out. He cannot put them in proper order when told to execute a "z out" pattern. Basketball: (1) A player repeats the commands for a particular play out of order. (2) A player has the skills to rebound, pass, and run but cannot put them in order for a fast break. Baseball: A shortstop can remember where to make a throw, but given a prioritized list of three choices for a particular situation, only randomly picks the correct choice.

In all sports good vision is an essential necessity. In many cases poor vision can cause serious injury. Many factors contribute to what is called vision. A problem with visual acuity is the easiest to detect simply because it becomes the most obvious. The athlete does not have the ability to see clearly and differentiate objects in the visual field. Many who wear corrective lenses normally assume that they can compensate athletically without glasses or contact lenses. Some even believe that corrective lenses will impede performance. Even in a sport like swimming, the ability to clearly see the black cross at the end of a pool can mean a significant difference in the flip turn. Football: (1) a receiver who demonstrates all other necessary skills has the ball continuously contact the hands slightly off target. (2) A quarterback in practice, where there are no numbers on jerseys, has trouble identifying who the various receivers were down field. (3) A punt receiver cannot identify which way the ball was spinning on a ball kicked to him. Basketball: (1) A player that two years previously was hitting certain shots from the field, can no longer hit with the same accuracy, and there appears to be no other causes.

(2) A player misreads or completely misses hand signals from the coach on the bench. (3) A player's passes always appear slightly off target. Baseball: (1) A batter complains of not being able to see the pitch well. (2) A pitcher misreads the catcher's signals.

A person suffering from poor visual coordination and pursuit has difficulty following and tracking objects. Many specialists in the field of vision training are now taking a much closer look at this disability from an athletic standpoint. Obviously, a superior athlete at a skill position cannot have a severe deficit, but in many cases the deficit may be present and have been well compensated for by the athlete's other skills. Football: (1) A quarterback who has beautiful fluidity of movement in throwing, good footwork, and appears to throw well in practice, but cannot pick up his receivers in a game situation. (2) A punt receiver claims he loses the ball in midair. (3) A linebacker continually has trouble adjusting his angle of pursuit. Basketball: (1) A player does not lead his teammates well when passing the ball. (2) A player is usually in the wrong place for a rebound. (3) A player's eyes are not following the shot smoothly. Baseball: (1) A runner misjudges the timing on a steal attempt. (2) A catcher has trouble with curve balls or sliders. (3) An outfielder never quite judges a fly properly.

The athlete with a visual form discrimination problem would be difficult to identify because the problem would be so subtle. That person would not be able to visually differentiate what would be normal to others. The athlete standing behind a play and watching it who cannot tell the coach the difference between correct and incorrect position might have this problem. In athletics it would be more of a problem of not being able to see a difference in various positions than it would the academic like and dislike symbols. For instance, not remembering whether a person was right-handed or left-handed after one pitch would indicate a possible problem.

In athletics a problem with visual figure-ground differentiation might be confused with one of visual coordination and pursuit because the results are often the same. As previously discussed, the person with a problem in visual coordination and pursuit loses the object. The operative term is loses, since this means the object was sighted to start. The individual with a visual figure-ground differentiation problem cannot pick up the object visually to start. The primary object is not readily distinguished from objects in the foreground and background. Football: (1) A linebacker is not able to visually pick up a running back coming out of the backfield. (2) A defensive back has difficulty seeing receivers coming into his zone. (3) A quarterback has problems picking out the open receiver in the field. Basketball: (1) A player does not see his teammates on a full court press. (2) A player has difficulty seeing his teammates when inbounding the ball. (3) A player does not see a defensive player at the moment of a pass and has the ball stolen.

Oftentimes a problem is one of visual memory. Not being able to learn from videos or film may be a problem in this area. The athlete cannot recall accurately from prior visual experience. That prior experience may be short-term or long-term. A good question to ask is, "What did you see that made you do that?" If the individual cannot respond, then visual memory may need remediation. In all sports the problem would basically present in the same fashion. The athlete would have trouble learning visually. From an athletic perspective visual memory and visual-motor memory are the same skill. Technically, visual-motor memory is the ability to reproduce, motor-wise, prior visual experiences. In many cases the athlete who has looked at the playbook cannot repeat those plays on the field. A playbook is virtually useless for the athlete with a visual-motor memory deficit. Probably from this single area, more than any other, comes the abusive rhetoric about not studying hard enough, not caring about the team, not being dedicated, or any number of other cliches. The sideline of any football or basketball game is filled with coaches diagramming adjustments for the team. To the frustration of the coach and the player these adjustments are not made, or in some cases are made only intermittently as a coincidence. The lack of consistency is what becomes so perplexing.

By definition, visual-motor spatial-form manipulation problems arise when an individual cannot successfully move in space and manipulate three-dimensional materials. For the athlete the term used quite often is "bad judgment." Football: (1) A running back replies that he thought the opening was easily large enough for him to run through, but he gets tackled solidly. (2) A quarterback throws over the heads of receivers, or, when he does complete passes, they are high. (3) A defensive lineman takes the wrong path to the quarterback on a pass rush and gets blocked easily. Basketball: (1) A player on defense keeps getting picked off thinking she can slide through the pick. (2) A player inbounds over the heads of teammates. (3) A player bounces his pass too close to defensive players and has the pass stolen. Baseball: (1) An infielder has trouble splitting the distance between two other players. (2) A batter places the bat too high whenever attempting a bunt. (3) A runner consistently slides too late to make it safely under a tag.

Visual-motor fine muscle coordination would only be apparent in the difference between average, good, and great athletes. Because athletics consists mostly of gross motor skills, many athletes can compensate easily for a difficulty in this area. But subtleties, such as the "soft hands" of a great receiver or the "quick hands" of a great shortstop, are apparent when dealing with an elite group. Most often on the lower levels there is not even the time to work on the very minute details of performance.

Visual motor integration is simply the ability to put it all together. It would be relatively safe to say that an athlete could not function with such an impairment. So much of athletics depends upon visual integration that disruption of any one of the previously discussed visual areas becomes a great concern. As has been stated previously, the athlete who is learning disabled is usually marginally impaired, whereas this category would constitute a gross impairment.

Language development as a complete area would not have the same impact on an athlete that the perceptual area had. Deficiencies in language development, while certainly detracting from the overall performance, would not have the direct effect on the gross or fine motor task. A deficient vocabulary would not allow the athlete to communicate well, either as the receiver or as the communicator. The same would be true of fluency and encoding. Since much of athletics involves the process of interpersonal communication, articulation difficulties can present a barrier. Most often this subarea takes the form of a dialect problem. Such dialects as Southern, Mountain, Western, Black, Oriental, Latino, and Brooklynese create difficulties with those unaccustomed to their particular sounds. Generally, once others are used to the sound, no further difficulties arise. The combined subareas of word attack skills, reading comprehension, writing, and spelling pose problems for the athlete required to utilize written instructions as a learning tool or an evaluative process. This would be a primary example of indirect interference with skill development. One should note that, although motor skills may not appear significantly impacted, processing problems in the language center of the brain may occur in conjunction with other neurological deficits which might otherwise remain undetected.

Conceptual skills are a big part of most sports. There are always uses for numbers, whether it be for counting, measuring, timing, scoring, or sequencing. Consider that "split right, 62, fake 34 across, 323 fly" is only one offensive play out of possibly one hundred that a player must learn in football. Including variations from different sets, right and left, strong and weak, there might easily be several hundred possibilities of plays — all dependent upon an individual's conceptual skills for execution.

A problem in number concepts, arithmetic process, or arithmetic reasoning would create such problems as discussed above. Though academically these three areas are distinguishable, athletically they simply present as an inability to use numbers regularly needed in the sport. Football: (1) An outside linebacker is told to take a 2×2 walkaway position but lines up incorrectly. (2) A receiver is told to drive seven steps to the outside shoulder of the defender, plant the inside foot, and come back two steps but cannot perform the proper number of steps to get the correct pattern. (3) On the kick-off return unit a player is told to block the third man from the left sideline, but is never able to identify the correct person. Basketball: (1) A player is not able to readily convert six shots from the field and two free throws into the corresponding number of points. (2) A player who is told to position himself two-thirds of the way down the court on a full court press is unable to locate the area. (3) A player who is told she has a vertical leap of 14 inches is unable to convert the figure into feet and inches. Baseball: (1) A batter who had three hits for four at-bats is unable to determine his batting average. (2) A player is unable to convert the standard 7 to 6 to 3 of baseball scoring into language terminology. (3) A batter cannot choke up one fourth of the way on the bat.

Classification and comprehension are also closely tied together from an athletic perspective. The ability to recognize relationships and to use logical judgment and reasoning in common sense situations is an integral part of sport. Many times these judgments need to be made instantaneously. The great runner who is able to decide between three choices of holes to run in football possesses superior skills in these areas. The baseball player who, in midair, fakes a throw one way then throws opposite to pick off a runner has great classification and comprehension skills related to his or her sport. Deficits in these areas are usually lumped together under the heading of "bad judgment" or "no feel for the game." Not being able to take advantage of an opponent's weaknesses because of judgmental errors rather than skill errors would indicate a deficiency in these areas. When basic skills are present but practical application is incorrect, an evaluation of logical relationships and comprehension is in order. Football: (1) A quarterback throws to the covered receiver as opposed to the open receiver. (2) A punt returner elects not to fair catch a ball even when opposing players are within close proximity. (3) When two players have entered a zone, the defensive back covers the wrong one, resulting in a completion for long yardage. Basketball: (1) A player does not take a shot when he is supposed to do so. (2) A player dribbles when she should have passed. (3) Late in the game a player tries a low percentage shot resulting in the other team scoring. Baseball: (1) A player goes for a double play when only one out is needed. (2) A runner tries to stretch a single into a double, resulting in an out. (3) An outfielder tries to throw home instead of hitting the cut-off man.

Especially in team sports, coaches strive toward esprit de corp. Yet, there are those whose social skills keep them outside of the circle, and they, as well as the team, do not benefit from any natural skills. The social psychology of athletics has already been discussed, and the social skill disability needs to be examined in the context of sport. Because sport is an intensified microcosm of society, social skills are continually scrutinized. Authorities in the field of learning disabilities such as Osman (65:61) suggest that disabilities in the academic areas of perceptual, language development, or conceptual skills are also often accompanied by a social skill dysfunction. While most of the time this is a result of another disability, it does, nonetheless, interfere and is therefore substantiated as a valid learning disability. Deficits in social skills often lead to psychopathologies.

The individual lacking in social acceptance is often isolated from the personal part of the team. He or she may have difficulty in a one-to-one relationship or in a group situation. Such factors as self-control and cooperation greatly influence the athlete's social acceptance. The first step is to identify those who are lacking in social acceptance, and the second is to look at specific situations in an attempt to determine the reasons for the problems. Small clues such as not running with the group on laps or being the object of negative comments or jokes would indicate a possible potential problem. This area is certainly more abstract than previously mentioned disabilities and requires that the person working with the athlete be highly intuitive.

The lack of good anticipatory response may in some ways be regarded as a conceptual disability in that logical inference is in question. Lack of anticipatory response can often precipitate a denial of social acceptance.

A lack of good value judgments may also bring about a lack of social acceptance. The athlete needs to have a sense of right and wrong, control his or her own behavior and aid in team behavior, and demonstrate appropriate behaviors when needed. A disability in this area is exemplified by the athlete who shows no respect for a teammate's possessions. One finds that often one person with a disability will berate another with a disability instead of demonstrating an understanding. This is tied together closely with a lack of social maturity, which is basically having appropriate value judgments at the appropriate chronological age. The social intelligence quotient is the social skills age divided by the chronological age. When the result falls too far below one, social problems, such as social acceptance, can be anticipated.

It should be recognized that one incident, as described in all previous examples of various problems, does not constitute a disability. However, the astute clinician will at least examine the possibility because of the rapidity of sport. Others working with the athlete should at least keep track of occurrences and refer them when necessary. A clue as to a particular disability may not appear again for awhile. It is only when a pattern has been observed that one can formulate a diagnosis.

Certainly to be included in any discussion of disabilities among athletes is the role of the coach. Most coaches would be able to describe what has thus far been discussed. In fact, examples cited were from coaches' personal observations. However, not realizing that these observed factors constitute a disability, coaches may be reluctant to take time to correct them, or at least to seek remediation for the problem from the appropriate source. And time is the basis for most problems, especially at the lower levels of athletic performance. A not-so-uncommon situation is one which oftentimes confronts coaches in so-called minor sports. Not having an off-season program, the coach meets for the first time with the team during the semester of competition. Well over half the people on the team are new. In three weeks' time, actually thirteen school days, paperwork has to be cleared, eligibility has to be checked, equipment has to be issued, skills have to be taught, rules of the game have to be taught, workouts have to be explained, injuries must be discussed, sportsmanship and team effort need to be discussed, newly taught skills need to be corrected, preparations need to be made for the first competition, all names of new people need to be learned, talent of rookies and veterans needs to be evaluated, and people need to be placed according to skill level. In many school districts this is all done by one coach with no assistants. To do one visual acuity test on each individual would take 2-3 days. In short, to evaluate each individual thoroughly is an impossibility.

If one were to ask any coach if he or she would like to get the most out of every athlete, they would most emphatically reply in an affirmative fashion. But for someone in sports to act, the results of any effort must be transformed into the bottom line, the athlete's performance. Unless it can be effectively demonstrated that these efforts will impact a player's performance, it is difficult to justify to a coach how an hour of testing and evaluation of learning disabilities can possibly be of at least equivalent value to an hour of skill work.

CASE REVIEWS — THE ATHLETE'S COPING STRATEGIES

While the following case histories do not depict all of the disabilities, they certainly present an illustration of the effects of a disability upon someone involved in sport. It should again be noted that these are problems that heretofore have gone unnoticed by the clinical community as they relate to athletics.

Student A: A's father was a classic example of the athletic parent who is reliving his past vicariously through his child. The father brought him to school to tell the coaching staff what a gem they had. *A* had distinguished himself in Pop Warner football as an outstanding athlete. His first two years of high school were spent at the Bee level, designed for smaller and younger boys, before moving to the varsity level for his senior year. Because of his abilities, the Bee coaches had plays that were simply designed to hand him the ball and "let him do his thing." Academically, *A*'s records were mixed. In certain classes he performed in an exemplary fashion, receiving high grades in some top academic subjects, while in other classes his performance was abysmally poor. Many teachers were frustrated and complained that he was basically lazy, only working when he felt the need. As a varsity player, *A* began to have problems. He seemed to continuously err both in practice and games to the point where he was benched. These errors were puzzling to the coaching staff since he always appeared to be studying his playbook, and, even on the field, appeared deeply engrossed in trying to study the plays. *A* had not faced this frustration previously because his natural talents had allowed everyone to make adjustments for him, but now he could not adjust. After three weeks, *A*'s problem was carefully observed. It became apparent that *A* ran in the wrong direction approximately 75 percent of the time. If a play was called left, he went right. If he was supposed to lift his right elbow for a hand-off, he lifted his left. Even his footwork appeared to be reversed.

At this point he was ridiculed by team members for being seventeen years old and not knowing his right from his left. *A* was asked by one of the coaches to read, upon suspicion of dyslexia. The usual letters were all reversed. *A* did not have the ability to listen to or see a play designed to run right or left and to execute that play. No one in eleven years of his football career had ever diagnosed the problem, though it was subsequently learned that he had been diagnosed academically.

The problem was a combination of a number of disabilities. Perceptually, the problems were auditory vocal-association, visual-form discrimination, and visual-motor memory. Conceptually, the significant problem was classification. The problem that resulted was one on social acceptance that became quite pronounced. No one had ever bothered to inform the coaches that *A* had an academic learning disability, and *A* never realized that his athletic performance was being affected. From that point on the coaches taped an "R" on his right shoe and right wrist and taped an "L" to his left shoe and left wrist. After having been benched for three weeks, *A* returned to the starting team and proceeded to break two school rushing records, be named the team's most valuable offensive back for the year, and to be named to the all-league squad. His social acceptance problem came to an abrupt end.

Student B: *B* had no prior history of any significance in sports. Throughout his elementary and junior high school years he was overweight. His self-image was poor, compounded by his apparent failure at academics. He was approximately three years behind grade level at the time of entering high school. *B*'s socialization skills were below average, and he was viewed as a buffoon by classmates. His swimming skills were reasonable, and as a result, he joined the high school swim team. The order of events was carefully explained and each student was given a copy of the order of events. In the first meet of the year *B* missed his first event. It was assumed that he was fooling around to the point of not concentrating on the meet. Because he missed one event, it was necessary by rules to remove him from all his scheduled events. The results cost the team the meet. Everyone concerned was quite annoyed, and *B* was chided harshly for his lack of team spirit. Two subsequent events led to a discovery of *B*'s learning disabilities as they related to athletics. The Special Day Curriculum (SDC) teacher made contact so that a proper Individual Educational Program (IEP) form could be filled out. This was the first notification that he had any problems. Second, it became apparent that under the stress of physical exertion *B* could not remember the order of the individual medley, although he could adequately perform each stroke. After careful evaluation, *B* was diagnosed as having a number of learning disabilities relating to athletics.

In the perceptual area he was deficient in both auditory memory and auditory sequencing, the reasons for missing events and not remembering the proper order. His language skills, particularly reading comprehension, were below average, Socially, he lacked good anticipatory response and was quite perplexed when confronted by teammates. This resulted in a problem with social acceptance. *B* was unable to master the skill of auditory memory.

The problem was dealt with by assigning other individuals in the same events the job of making sure *B* checked in at the proper time. The sequencing problem was more difficult. In practice someone stood at the wall to yell the proper stroke after each two laps. This technique, combined with good effort on *B*'s part, allowed him to comprehend the proper order in both the medley relay and the individual medley. The socialization process did not meet with the same degree of success initially. It took almost two full seasons for his social skills to become adequate. *B*'s athletic abilities never led to any significant heights, but his efforts did give him the necessary positive reinforcement to attain good social growth.

Student C: As a young child, *C* was always one of the most physically adept individuals. Much of his popularity could be accounted for because he was wanted on everyone's team. Through his elementary and junior high school years *C* received poor grades but was always passed on. Even his academic records made no mention of any special needs. His teachers labelled him lazy and apathetic. *C* was the star of his youth football teams, even though most of his coaches referred to him as "uncoachable" but likeable. He rarely had a personality conflict with anyone. In fact, he had a wide circle of friends. *C*'s talents at the high school level were immediately apparent. He was faster and stronger than other running backs, and he had good hands and great balance, as well. In preseason drills he was an obvious standout.

Playbooks were distributed, and, prior to each practice, chalk talks (informal discussions of the plays) were conducted. *C* consistently made errors during the plays, sometimes running the wrong pattern, going to the wrong hole, or blocking the wrong man. However, when he did get the ball, *C* was a superb runner. He was told he was selfish for not learning the plays or blocking for the other running backs. After being demoted to second team for two weeks, *C* approached the coaching staff. He stated that he truly did not understand the playbook and that when plays were talked about he became completely confused. Upon diagnosis, *C* was discovered to have multiple disabilities.

Perceptually, he was lacking in auditory-vocal association, auditory memory, auditory sequencing, and visual form discrimination. The reading comprehension aspect of language was quite poor. Conceptually, *C* had poor arithmetic reasoning and classification skills, in simplest terms he had difficulty learning from both an auditory and visual model. *C* was referred to the appropriate instructional program where academic testing confirmed the suspected weaknesses. The solution to *C*'s problems was to walk him through each play. The results were remarkable. He made virtually no mistakes after walking through a given play only once. Corrections or modifications were also done in the same fashion. During the course of the semester *C* also received much help academically. He made substantial progress toward the goal of functioning at grade level.

Chapter Four

BRUCE JENNER—THE STRUGGLE WITH HIS LEARNING DISABILITY

IN 1976 Bruce Jenner culminated his amateur athletic career with a gold medal in the Olympic Games for his performance in the decathlon. For that he was considered the top male athlete in the world for that year. Few people knew of his struggle to compensate for his learning disability and how this affected his athletic performance. He became the first big name in athletics to acknowledge that he had a learning disability.

The authors are grateful to Bruce Jenner for allowing them to share his story so that others in similar situations may find hope and encouragement in their endeavors. Rather than paraphrase a sensitive and personal account, the authors felt that Bruce Jenner's own words best expressed his struggle to improve his own self-image and to cope with his learning disability. It is the expression of how one person changed a liability into a big asset, and made the most out of a difficult problem. The following is the dialogue between the authors and Bruce Jenner.

Authors: How do you feel about sharing your story with others?

Bruce: I feel an obligation to help out as much as I can because when I was growing up it was tough. It wasn't easy. I was fortunate enough to find something through sports that gave me a big lift. I'd like to try and help kids out.

Authors: I've had a number of kids over the years with some problems. When you came out in the L.A. Times with the quotation about how rough it had been on you, it meant a lot to the kids.

Bruce: The first thing I did was many years ago, probably eight years ago. I had just never talked about this because nobody had ever brought the subject up. Everybody thinks that because you go out and win the game that your whole life has been perfect. I did a thing with Dr. William Rader on T.V. But I really hadn't done much since no one had asked me any questions. I did this piece for the local news, and I got probably more letters from a local news thing than anything I'd ever done. I said, "My gosh, I guess there's a need for it out there. Since then I've tried to do as much as I can.

Authors: *At what age did you realize that you had a problem learning?*

Bruce: As best as I can recollect, probably first grade-ish. I had two things at that age. One, I didn't like school. I cried, screamed, and didn't want to go to school. Secondly, I had a perceptual problem with just picking things up off the paper. The combination of the two made me sort of sit at the back of the class and want to go to sleep all the time. I would just totally avoid what was going on.

Authors: *So your way of coping with the problem was avoiding it.*

Bruce: At first. I was left back in second grade. I could have gone to school at four, just turning five, or at five, just turning six. My parents decided to go with four turning five. So I was one of the younger kids in the class. When it came to second grade, I wasn't doing very well, my attention span was really low, I wasn't doing that well in school, so they decided to hold him back. Maybe it will give him another year to mature. That was one way for them to deal with the problem, but they really had no idea what the problem was. We're talking back in the fifties. At that time they really didn't look for learning disabilities. Nowadays they look out for kids who are dyslexic or having other types of learning disabilities. Holding me back in the second grade might have helped a little bit by making me grow up, but it didn't help the whole situation. Probably, it hurt me in a lot of ways, too, because of the shame of being a young kid, being in the second grade, and being held back another year. You have to tell your friends that. That certainly didn't help me with my self-image. It was really in the third, fourth, and fifth grades that I was always in the slower classes. I always had a problem with reading. My biggest fear, at those ages, was to have to read in front of the class. That's the hardest thing I've ever done in my life. I'd hate to go to school. I'd go with sweaty palms and scared to death just because I was afraid I would have to read in front of a class. I didn't like that.

Authors: *At what point during your schooling did somebody let you know that it was a very specific problem and identify it for you so that you could begin to understand it a little bit more?*

Bruce: The first time I can remember anybody ever saying anything was in junior high school. I was probably in the seventh grade. At that point, because I had a perceptual problem, they thought that dealing with it was getting a pair of glasses. Maybe you had bad vision. So I went to a doctor, got some prescription, and got some glasses made which didn't help at all. That was not the problem. Also at that time they came up with the label of dyslexia. They just gave it a name. I never took any special classes. They didn't do anything else except give me a label. This was in a public school. I never went to any specialized school. I wasn't a problem kid. I was the nice kid. I was always the teacher's pet. I wasn't a discipline problem or anything like that. I was just slow. Because of the reading, it made me slow in everything. I could do the work, but it was real frustrating for me, so I avoided it. I was just doing enough to get by.

Authors: *So you were really struggling at home just in the own secrecy of your house.*

Bruce: Yes. I also grew up with a sister who was the real genius. She was a year and four months older than I was and two years ahead of me in school. She studied four hours a night. And I put in fifteen minutes.

Authors: *So you got pressure from all the teachers about the older sister.*

Bruce: Oh, yes. Definitely. It wasn't until junior high school, and really in high school that I started playing in sports. That was a big change.

Authors: *Did you turn to that because you were getting good strokes from it?*

Bruce: That's exactly what I did. I remember in fifth grade being in a running relay where you had to time yourself around these chairs up and back, up and back. I had the fastest time in the school. That was really the first time that I realized that this was sort of fun. Then in junior high school I went out for wrestling and developed a knee problem and all through junior high wasn't even able to play in the gym class. It wasn't until I was a freshman in high school that I started getting more seriously interested in sports.

Authors: *What did you play in high school?*

Bruce: Football, basketball, and ran track. I also competitively water skiied all summer long. I did the water skiing from when I was about fourteen until I was about twenty-one.

Authors: *Is there anyone else in your family, parents or children, that has any learning problems?*

Bruce: No, I haven't noticed any of my four kids having any problems. My five-year-old does better with words than I did in fifth grade, and he's just entering kindergarten. They say that some learning disabilities can be inherited and I'm very aware of it, so I keep an eye on these things. But I haven't noticed any problem whatsoever.

Authors: *How did your problem with learning disabilities interfere, if at all, with your athletics?*

Bruce: I don't think it interfered as far as reading playbooks or something like that. I could do the work, but, one, it was frustrating for me, and two, it took me longer. If I had this burning desire to read this playbook, because I wanted to play on the football team, I read it. And I struggled through it. As far as reading my history assignment, that didn't thrill me at all. Different motivation. Basically, what I needed at that point was confidence in myself. I had no confidence in myself. I had a very low image of myself, intellectually. At that age we base our self worth in life on how we're doing in school, about how good of grades we're getting, marks on tests, and all those things. That's how we judge ourselves and whether we're going to be a good human being or not, if we're going to make it in life. A lot of people put a lot of pressure on you to do well. I wasn't getting the good feelings. All of a sudden with sports I could lift my head up high. I could go out on the football field with a guy who is getting "A's" on tests and be right up there with him, and in most cases beat him. That makes you feel pretty good about yourself. So when you walk down the hall in school you can raise your head up high.

Authors: *Were any of the coaches sensitive to the fact that you had difficulties or help you with it?*

Bruce: No. Never that I can remember.

Authors: *Did they even understand if you said you were having trouble reading any of the playbooks? Were there any of the comments that you weren't studying it hard enough?*

Bruce: No. I was a smart kid. I realize that now. I wasn't dumb. I could memorize things because I had to. I was forced to memorize things. And so you develop your skill of memorization. I might have a hard time reading, but once I read it and got it in my little head, it was there. And it stayed. It wasn't that I was dumb. I didn't realize that I was smart, but if I wanted to do something, I could do it. If I seriously wanted to get an "A" on a test, I did. I just didn't care about that. A lot of it was the attitude that I had developed in the first to fourth grades. I got a bad start, and it put me behind all the time. My form of dyslexia was not so severe that I couldn't learn. I could do the work. It was just really slow and tedious. And I didn't want anyone to know that I had the problem.

Authors: *Then your form of dyslexia is a visual dyslexia.*

Bruce: Yes. I'll briefly explain how it is. My eyes work fine. My brain works fine. There's just a little short circuit in between. I can be reading along, picking things up off the paper, and all of a sudden things just don't come very quickly. It could be a big, long, complicated word or it could be a simple word like "is" or "the." But all of a sudden things just don't want to register. I can see it, but it takes a beat for it to start to register what it is. When I was younger and had to read in front of the class, I got so nervous, I would be reading along for four or five words but then all of a sudden one word wouldn't want to come up off the paper. I would struggle with it and get frustrated, embarrassed, and my palms would start sweating, and the whole process went right out the window. I couldn't do it after that.

Authors: *Was the term "dumb jock" from any of the teachers or anyone else ever applied?*

Bruce: Not "dumb jock" but "slow jock." I think most of my teachers might have thought I was slow, but I don't think any of them thought I was dumb. In areas like science where I didn't have to read, I would come up with good stuff. But if I had to write it down on a piece of paper or read it off a piece of paper, I'd have a hard time with it. Once the teachers explained it, I could get it. I probably considered myself the dumb jock more than the people that I was involved with. It was more my perception of myself.

Authors: Did these conflicts create any psychological problems for you such as socialization, depression, or anything similar?

Bruce: Definitely. I had some depression. But the depression was more before I found sports. I didn't socialize that much when I was younger. As I got into junior high and high school and all of a sudden I found sports, I had something. Every little kid growing up needs a pat on the back. They need somebody, some adult, some peer, somebody to come up and say, "Hey, you did a good job!" Everybody needs that. I wasn't getting it in my schoolwork, but all of a sudden when I found sports, I could get that. As I walked down the hall, I could hold my head up high. When you're the big star of the football team, everybody loves you. Or you go out there and score thirty points in the basketball, all of a sudden everybody loves you. Because of that, the schoolwork became less, and I just tried to hide that. I was always in the slower classes and I was always embarrassed by that. I was with the kids that I didn't feel that I fit in with. But I knew I deserved to be there. In the fifth or sixth grade they took me out of the slow class and put me in the regular class. That was a big, big deal for me because I didn't like being associated with the slower class. Everybody knew that was the slow class. When they let me out of that into another class, it was like "Wow! This is great!" It took me a little bit longer, but I could do the work in the regular classes. But I also think maybe I tried a little bit harder.

Authors: So you were feeling better about yourself.

Bruce: Yes. When you feel bad about yourself, it creates other problems. I remember in junior high school they let me go on the safety patrol where you monitor the stairs. That was a big deal for me. The teachers had given me enough responsibility that I could be on the safety patrol. All the other kids on the safety patrol were always in the faster classes, always sort of the big time people, the good students. And here I was one of them. Things like that really meant a lot.

Authors: *So right now you really understand your disability. You can talk about it and have a good grasp.*

Bruce: Yes. I've lived it for thirty-seven years. And I know my limitations. I still have the problem. What I don't have now is the problem with confidence in myself. I know I can do the work. I still have problems with reading. I am not a good reader by anybody's standards. But I can go on Good Morning America and sub in for David Hartman and read large amounts of copy in front of millions and millions of people. I could not do that thirty years ago. I couldn't read in front of my class. You don't grow out of it. You just learn to live around it. For me its almost like a big scam. Nobody knows I have the problem. I know what I have to do to get around it. I go in a little early, get all the copy in advance that's going to be on the teleprompter, and I study my little buns off. I know that I can do the work. Secondly, I can memorize it really fast. I can take a sixty second piece of copy and read it through three or four times, and underline key words. As long as I know the structure of the sentence and the paragraph, and where everything is going, I'll have it down so good that I get in there and read that prompter. It may not come off exactly as it was written, but if you're on the outside looking in, you would never know it because I can fill in all the spaces and I've memorized where the paragraph is going. To me, that's one of the more fun things to do. It's probably about twenty percent ad libbing and eighty percent getting it off the paper and memorizing it. If I didn't know where the paragraph was going, I'd be in trouble. The first couple of times I read through it I'm struggling. I read through it and take it word for word and go through it slowly and put it in my little memory bank. If I had to read that thing cold, I'd be in big trouble.

Authors: *If you're talking about athletes with learning disabilities, and you're Bruce Jenner, what would you tell them?*

Bruce: First of all, it doesn't have to be athletics for a kid with learning disabilities. That is just one form of something that you can do.

What I suggest for kids is to find some area in their lives. When God made you, He took away in one area. Maybe in my case or another person's case it was being dyslexic and having a reading problem and perception problem. If He took it away in that area, He didn't take away your whole life. That's only one area of your life. Then you're going to get even more in another area. What you have to do is find that area. It can be in athletics. It can be in the arts. It can be in dance or music. It can be in many, many areas. But find them. Let's take my area of athletics. Use that as a confidence builder in your life. Get the confidence that you can go out, perform, and then come back and do some of the others and conquer some of the other problems. The other things can be conquered. You can conquer them in the sense that you can live with them and live a good life with them. Once you find those areas and you start to gain some confidence in yourself, you start to hold your head up high, you start to feel good about yourself. Use those strengths. The exact same things that you used to get ahead in that area, are the same things you're going to use to get ahead and learn to read better. Its all the same thing. Its hard work, dedication, and practice. And then you have that performance that you have to give. And under the heat of the battle, in athletics you learn this really fast, you just go out and do your thing. Its the same thing in reading. You have to learn the basics. Maybe don't call it practice, call it homework. It's a confidence thing. And then there is the performance where you may have to read in front of the class. You have to muster up all your courage and get out there and put it on the line.

Authors: *Knowing what you know right now about your disability, what would you have changed as you were growing up?*

Bruce: Not a thing, to be honest with you. I think because of my problems in getting started in school, which had a tremendous impact on me, I have a good attitude. I know now this is a problem that I can live with. This is not the end of the world. Growing up I think it created a confidence problem, but I think because of that, and because of getting involved with sports, I'm a better person. Honestly, I don't think I would change anything. That was a character builder, just growing up with this problem. If it was easy in school, school was going great, I was sort of just sliding through, I could get an "A," and read well, I might not have been that hot on athletics because I wouldn't need it. I would have been doing fine on my own. As things got more intense with track and field, I had such drive to succeed, to do well, and to hopefully pull off the games. I don't think I would have had that drive if I had an easy upbringing.

Authors: *So you turned what could have been a liability into a good asset.*

Bruce: Yes, it definitely was. My biggest strength in my athletic career, my number one asset, the one I depended on every time I went out on the field, was my mental capacity. I was stronger mentally than any athlete out there, and I knew it. It's funny, because here's a kid who grew up dyslexic and didn't have any confidence in himself intellectually, goes out into a sport and his number one asset years down the line is the ability to think under pressure, to be able to come up with performances when I needed it, to be able to do exactly what I needed to do to win. I learned that through going through performances of success, of failure, in all these different areas. When it came down to the biggest pressure of my competition, the Games, I knew I was stronger mentally than any person out there. And I knew nobody was going to beat me, because if I had to come up with a performance, it was going to be there. Physically, I had done all the work, and mentally I could get it out of me. Throw more pressure on me, I don't care. The biggest pressure meets of the year were always the ones that I did better in. For me, pressure was something that was very positive. It's something that was going to make my brain turn on. I was going to go out there, and I was going to come up with a performance. I consider the competition 80 percent a mental challenge and 20 percent a physical challenge. In the off-season or training it's the reverse. But the actual performance is a mental game. It's being able to come up with that performance at the right time.

Authors: *What advice would you give to people working with athletes who have learning disabilities? How would you tell them to do what it is that you did?*

Bruce: Be a friend. That's so very important, especially in an athletic situation where a kid comes in with no confidence in himself because of a learning problem in some area. They need someone to be a friend and give them some guidance. Give them a chance. Some people think that a kid who has learning disabilities cannot accept a challenge. Give them a chance. Give them a physical and mental challenge and see how they do. Just the little successes like my being on safety patrol or being moved up in a class are very big things to that person. Somebody out there took a chance with me and saw possibilities deep down inside. I would get that, and I would thrive on that. In athletics they sometimes don't think a kid can handle it. In a safe situation where it's not going to hurt the team effort, give him a little responsibility. Don't give up the first time, because the first time they're going to be nervous as heck. Be there when they need you the most.

It is the authors' hope, as well as that of Mr. Bruce Jenner, that his story serves as an inspiration to all those with learning disabilities. Provided with the right atmosphere and motivation, the disabilities may be dealt with in a positive fashion. The key element is the self. Those working with the individual need to "be there when needed" to provide the support system necessary for the individual to succeed. Not everyone can go on to win a gold medal in the Olympics, but hopefully every person with a learning disability can, as Bruce Jenner so appropriately states, live a good life.

Chapter Five

REMEDIATING AND COMPENSATING FOR LEARNING DISABILITIES IN ATHLETICS

WHAT NEEDS to be emphasized again is that any one incident described previously does not necessarily mean that a disability is present. When a new set of diagnostic tools becomes available, the tendency is to label everyone as falling into one of the categories. This is certainly not the intent, and information garnered should be used judiciously. As experts in the field of learning disabilities have already concluded, many of the problems will not be remediated. What needs to be accomplished is the development of adequate coping strategies so that compensation becomes an easier process. It should also be strongly emphasized that much of the responsibility of practicing the remediating and compensating strategies need to be assumed by the athlete, supported by coaches, parents, and professionals.

One of the most effective means of instruction is to present a multisensory approach to promote the desired skill. As an example, a football player learning a particular play should be given instructions verbally, be given a play sheet, copy the play from the chalkboard, walk through the play, and be explained how this particular part fits into the overall scheme. From a performance aspect, this multisensory approach insures several important things. First, it insures that the individual without disabilities, which will be the majority of the team, has a lot of repetition. Even though relatively free of any handicaps, most individuals have strengths and weaknesses where learning is concerned. Second, it allows for those who learn in a specific fashion. And third, it eliminates much of the time needed for correction. There will then be fewer athletes who do not understand. Time may be used to give additional instruction, using the proper learning mode, to those who are in need. Identifying the learning disabled athlete at an early stage alleviates much frustration on everyone's part.

No one is suggesting that a coach needs to become a resource specialist, but a reevaluation of teaching techniques may be in order for some. The realization and understanding of the disability is probably enough to put creative forces to work. The whole purpose of organized athletics is to have athletes reach the highest levels of individual potential. This sometimes requires innovative techniques.

The vast majority of athletes are not on the professional level. Most combine athletic endeavors with education. As difficult as it may be for some to accept, sports are only one aspect of life. The coach should be first and foremost an educator. As such, she or he has the obligation to produce not only top-notch athletes, but top-notch people. The influence that most coaches exert on their athletes is phenomenal. It should be the responsibility of the coach to ensure that if remediations made on the field can be carried into the classroom, they are done so promptly and properly.

With the advent of strictly enforced eligibility rules, the coach may not only be aiding the athlete in the classroom, but at the same time keeping that individual eligible. Even the National Collegiate Athletic Association has enacted new and stricter eligibility regulations.

The ability of the school system to screen for learning disabilities is limited. By simple observation the coach may discover something that has gone unnoticed for years. The results could benefit everyone involved. But the biggest concern should be for the individual.

In working with athletes who exhibit minimal to severe learning disabilities in the performance arena of their sport, the key factor to retain in the mind of the coach is compensating strategies. The disability may not always be remediated.

Within the auditory modality the focus is either on visual or motor compensation. Within the realm of auditory acuity, the emphasis needs to be on compensation, rather than remediation since no one can make provisions for louder auditory stimuli. Other players need to be made aware of the individual's deficit and can be utilized as the player's "ear." Officials can be warned that the player suffers from a hearing deficiency. The player must also be trained to pay closer attention to the officials. An athlete needs to be trained to watch the opponent's eyes and body more closely since the person cannot hear teammates signalling. Peripheral vision work needs to be done by the athlete. Athletes with a hearing loss need to pay closer attention to coaches' visual cues. The player should be drilled at various times during practice by, for example, holding a different number of fingers and having the player later tell how many, thereby getting them used to paying closer attention to the coaches.

If an athlete exhibits a deficit in auditory decoding, it is most critical to identify at which point the decoding is breaking down: initially, medially, or finally. Once this identification has been made the coach needs to make sure that the athlete is maintaining eye contact during administration of directions and, that as much as possible, directions are visual, involving symbols and color coding. Additionally, it would be paramount for the athlete to repeat back the directions administered so that the coach is assured of proper understanding on behalf of the athlete. Having a tape recorder to play back all the plays so that an athlete becomes familiar with the sounds associated with particular plays is an excellent strategy that has met with much success. The athlete may also work with another teammate, having the other repeating plays while the athlete responds with what he or she believes to be the proper physical actions.

In auditory vocal, auditory memory, and auditory sequencing deficits, visual and pictorial clues are essential to the athlete. This can be accomplished through cue cards or films so the athlete knows exactly what is expected. In combination with visual clues, walking the athlete or *motoring* the athlete through the plays or movement will help with patterning and retention of sequencing of the movements and actions. As with auditory decoding deficits, it is most important that the coach has the athlete repeat back the administered instructions so the coach is assured of understanding and processing of the information in the correct and proper order of application and implementation. The pattern of repetition needs to be consistent every day. Even one missed day can lead to a loss of memory. An excellent compensatory method is mnemonics. This is the process of taking the first letter of each word in a series and making a new nonsense word. As an example, the pass play "Right eighteen fly, Y up" becomes REFYUP. As imagined, the possibilities are limitless. Another compensatory strategy is visualization. Given the same play, the new "idea" would be to visualize an "R" eating (eighteen) a fly with a capital "Y" up. While appearing extreme initially, the whole procedure can be modified and streamlined to fit the particular needs of the team and sport.

Visual deficits present other types of problems for the athlete. When there exists a problem with visual acuity, the athlete simply needs to be made to understand that the corrective lenses prescribed need to be worn at all times, and that not wearing them will impede performance.

For deficiencies in visual coordination and tracking the use of a tachistoscope (a visual tracking instrument) and video games would be helpful for improving this skill. Through the advent of modern technology the video games have proven to be invaluable in visual tracking. The athlete using the video game would follow one object through the patterns of the game on the screen. It would also be important that the coach stress to maintain contact on the ball.

Those athletes experiencing difficulties with visual form discrimination in attempting to emulate the proper athletic position may benefit from matching their bodies up to a shadow image trying to duplicate their body position with the correct image of what is expected. Another valuable remediation would be to motor through the positions slowly in front of a mirror or video camera. The image desired could then be taped as a silhouette on the mirror so the athlete could then reduplicate this position. The same technique could also be duplicated on life size pieces of hard construction paper used as templates.

Two methods of dealing with visual figure-ground difficulties and directionality are films and varying backgrounds. Directionality for some athletes can be confusing and with momentary directions from a coach, the time to think and process the proper direction comes with a great cost. Keeping track of another athlete in the playing area presents problems for some athletes, this being tied closely with visual tracking. An athlete watching game or practice films of the sport will be asked to follow one particular player or object through the entire film. Then he or she will again watch the same film, but with a different assignment. This can be done until the athlete is able to follow any of the assigned players or objects through the film without difficulty. Backgrounds can be made artificially and varied to meet the needs of the situation. These can either be enlarged photographs or hand drawn (or computer drawn) pictures with varying color and object size.

Primarily with sports which require knowledge, memorization and retrieval of many different plays, visual memory and visualization of these plays are tantamount to the sport. For those athletes with poor visual memory other techniques for learning this information need to be employed. Color coding of the different stages and phases of the plays on paper or during chalk talks is one strategy so the athlete can visualize the plays. Converting the pictorial display to verbalization and taping it into a tape recorder can assist the athlete with a strong language base and good understanding of language. Converting the plays into manipulative symbols and reconstructing and manipulating the visal symbols and pictures may help to imprint this information into the memory. The athlete may also want to motor through each play using the actual area on which the game is played. A game of athletic concentration is very helpful in working on visual memory. Several plays would each be broken down into different parts, each part being placed on a separate index card. The cards would then be turned face down and mixed up. The athlete would then have to begin turning over one card at a time, not being allowed to leave the cards face up until all cards in a given play have been identified in order. In this manner the skill of visual memory is specific to the situation.

Anticipating and planning for the proper spatial area may present problems for those athletes with poor visual spatial skills. Actually working through spatial areas to duplicate what may be present on the playing field can assist the athlete in getting a feel for the space needed to be experienced. In addition, the concept of distance and the force required to move a ball from one position to another can be practiced by setting certain distances and trying to propel the ball, anticipating the proper required force. An obstacle course comprised of moving through varied spatial obstacles, as opposed to a physical fitness exercise, would aid the athlete. These should include crawling on the stomach and back, crawling on the hands and knees, and moving over, around, through, and under a variety of objects. Included in this exercise would be the verbalization of how large or small the space is.

Many sports require fine reasoning abilities on the part of the athlete. For those athletes who are deficient in this area actual reasoning skills need to be rehearsed and trained. The primary point of training should be related to the sport involved. Included within this training should be skills involving drawing conclusions and anticipating consequences of the actions in the playing arena. Players experiencing these types of deficits may need to verbally sequence the initiation of the play, the resultant actions, followed by the conclusions. Those athletes whose verbal skills are weak may perform these reasoning skills better by drawing them out or dramatizing them.

The basic academic skills of numbers and numerical concepts are essential for proper score keeping, implementation of plays and calculating movements. It is most important for the coach to know that the athlete has an understanding and knowledge of the basic mathematical operations of addition, subtraction, multiplication, division, fractions, percentages and decimals. It is also imperative that the athlete have an understanding of the concepts of "greater than" and "lesser than," and the relationship of numerical parts to the numerical whole. Deficits in any of these areas can interfere with understanding and implementations of directions and application to the sport. Motoring the athlete through activities requiring numerical concepts will aid in an understanding. However, since this area is mostly academic, the ideal would be to ensure the athlete be in a remedial math class or work with an educational therapist. However, the coach or assistant may design his or her own mini math course with the specifics of the sport as the basis for the work. As examples, down and distance or the counting down of the game clock are math procedures that need to be understood, and with practice there is a greater chance that the athlete will comprehend. Continuous repetition of ideas will also show beneficial results.

Chapter Six

AUXILIARY-RELATED PROBLEMS

WHILE this chapter may appear as a short course in abnormal psychology, it is intended only as a means to illustrate psychopathologies from an athletic perspective. This is something that has thus far not been done. Hopefully, not only the learning disabled athlete with a psychopathology will be diagnosed properly, but a new view of sports-related problems will be brought to light.

Because of the intensified atmosphere of sport, a learning disability may be the direct cause of a psychopathology, or a preexisting psychopathology may become magnified. It is, therefore, necessary that a familiarity with athletic psychopathologies be a part of the repertoire of the person working psychoeducationally with the learning disabled athlete.

In no other walk of life is the constancy of the public more prevalent than in the area of athletics. From the first time that an individual "gets ink" all the way up through the professional ranks, the lives and problems of athletes are continually dissected by the scalpels of the media. Virtually every newspaper has its own sports section, every television station its own sports segment, every major university its own amateur gladiators, and many large cities their professional gladiators. The reality is that America, and much of the world, takes its sports very seriously. Enter the athlete.

What precisely is expected and why does hitting a ball with a stick or throwing an odd-shaped ball 60 yards down field or throwing a ball through a hoop or smacking a ball with criss-crossed gut on a frame create problems where none existed and exacerbate those that already exist? The answers lay in a pressure cooker that intensifies and magnifies psychopathologies. To the layperson, baseball players damned well better be perfect for receiving $2 to 3 million per year. The win-at-all-costs ethic has created a tension that many cannot handle. The psychopathologies of athletics are a real part of the game that need to be dealt with. It has been stated abundantly that "athletics is up to 20 percent physical and at least 80 percent psychological," but the action of sports organizations on all levels does not reflect that addage.

Aggressive behavior and violence is generally frowned upon during the course of everyday living. Yet our society not only expects, but demands this pattern of behavior in athletes. Society politely calls it "intense competition." Yet when it is out of hand, there are no means of controlling it. DSM-III (5:6) conceptualizes mental disorders as being clinically significant if they create disability or distress. "Violent behavior," according to Edwin Megargee, "does not meet these criteria and is therefore not included as a mental disorder (1:523)."

The parameters of psychopathology need to be established. J.L. Phillips has given a functional definition of psychopathology that includes five criteria (67:101): the organism is unable to solve a problem or reach a goal; the organism persists in attempting to solve the problem; the organism lacks the immediate skills or means with which to solve the problem or reach the goal; the persistent or redundant efforts to reach the goal are not adaptive, resourceful, inventive, or effective; the redundant and maladaptive efforts to reach the goal bring about, or are associated with, maladaptive and unsuccessful behavior. This appears to be a specific definition of the terms "can't function" or "can't cope."

For the athlete the problem is then complicated by the idea that there is no time for, nor is there an acceptance of, a solution that is not immediate. If one is having trouble batting, the coach tells him or her to drop the elbow six inches, he drops it and proceeds to hit a home run. How simple! If she is having trouble with ninety thousand spectators screaming obscenities at her, then tell her something that she can do right now, because tomorrow someone else may have her position.

The psychopathologies discussed, while some athletes have other distinct problems, are some that have been observed over a fifteen-year span in coaching. The authors have attempted to concentrate on those aspects of abnormal personalities that they feel would be most evident in the practice of dealing with athletes from a psychological aspect. They include affective disorders, anxiety disorders, somatoform and factitious disorders, and personality disorders. It should be remembered that these are classifications used in DSM-III, and that rather than an attempt to compartmentalize all disorders relating to athletics into "neat little DSM packages," the terms are used as an initial starting point for discussion of sports-related psychopathologies. Hopefully, with more research and discussion the perspectives of those dealing with sports, psychology will impact the entire arena in a positive fashion.

There are those who would argue that these psychopathologies are no different than those appearing in the general population. In fact, most studies indicate that the athletic community, as a whole, has far fewer psychopathologies and is significantly better adjusted than the general population. While the idea is partially correct, it fails to take a closer look at the problem. The pathologies of athletes need to be viewed from a different perspective than what has thus far been used. To reiterate, the athlete does not have the time to engage in extensive therapies. This in and of itself sets the psychopathologies of athletics apart.

AFFECTIVE DISORDERS

"The essential features of this group of disorders is a disturbance of mood, accompanied by full or partial manic or depressive syndrome, that is not due to any other physical or mental disorder (5:205)." In general, we refer to manic or depressive as bipolar or unipolar.

As White and Watt comment, "Melancholia and mania have been recognized as forms of psychological disorder for more than two thousand years (95:521)." At the extremes, depressed states typically mean prolonged and seemingly senseless suffering for the person. Manic states may lead to unwise decisions and ultimately to exhaustion. Of course, carried to the extreme the results are psychosis, loss of reality. Part of that view is emphasized by Craighead et al., "Depression is a prevalent problem of personal and social significance (86:184)." Of the two areas, "Mania has been much less a target of inquiry (1:349)." Therefore, mania will be examined first.

The manic episode has the essential feature of a distinct period when the predominant mood is either elevated or expansive. Such concrete symptoms as hyperactivity, inflated self-esteem, and flight of ideas are usually present. The person may be loud and difficult to interrupt. If this sounds like a typical ego-inflated athlete, it may be. In some ways society has created this. It is also the authors' unproven hypothesis that the prolific use of cocaine may have its roots in the manic-depressive syndrome. Many of the effects of the drug mirror the described symptoms of the manic episode. The athlete can at least function under the manic episode, but not under the depressive side. Hence, the use is an attempt to keep the disorder as a unipolar-manic and still be able to perform. Of course, the consequences are still disastrous.

As Donland suggests, "Depression is an extremely common disorder which most people experience sometime during their lives. Normally it is related to life events (28:75)." The major features of the depressive episodes are usually a depressed mood and/or loss of pleasure in almost all usual activities. Specific symptoms include appetite disturbance, decreased energy feeling, loss of self-esteem, difficulty in concentration, and thoughts of death or suicidal attempts.

In athletics the term "psych-out your opponent" has a very real ring to it. Perhaps it should be "cause your opponent to suffer a major depressive episode" because, short of the suicide, the named symptoms are precisely what the athlete attempts to have happen to his or her opponent. This emphasizes the idea of 90 percent psychological and a mere 10 percent physical. It is a small wonder that some athletes suffer from bipolar affective disorders. If one closely examines DSM-III's criteria for a major depressive episode (5:213), he finds even more remarkable correlations to the everyday life of the athlete.

The first part of the criteria deals with a dysphoric mood or loss of pleasure, depressed, sad, blue, etc. The second area gives specific symptoms that must be present, four of eight: poor appetite or significant weight loss or severe weight gain; insomnia or hypersomnia; psychomotor agitation; loss of interest in usually pleasurable activities; loss of energy or fatigue; feelings of worthlessness or guilt; lack of concentration; and recurrent thoughts of death, suicidal ideation, wishes or attempts. What has just been described is the classic "slump" pattern that many athletes cyclically go through, including the idea of suicide. It was not too long ago that a star baseball pitcher calmly walked to the mound and proceeded to put an end to a brilliant career by "blowing his brains out" with a handgun. And more recently a female runner, realizing that she could not possibly win a race that she was expected to dominate, attempted to end her life by jumping off a bridge. She survived and is now crippled for the rest of her life. The comments by others close to the situation were that they were not surprised because of the pressure placed on all of them. Admittedly, more research needs to be performed, but why have very few professionals dealing with sports recognized slumps for what they are, in some cases, a major depressive episode. And that assessment would allow the situation to be treated as a psychopathology rather than "choking" as it is so affectionately called. Even the fan has to be educated that the condition is not the result of a "temperamental, overpaid baby who hasn't gotten his or her way."

ANXIETY DISORDERS

Spielberger, Pollous, and Worden label anxiety as "an unpleasant emotional state or reaction that can be distinguished from other emotions such as anger or grief by a unique combination of experiential qualities and physiological changes (86:263)." There generally exists tension, apprehension, nervousness, and worry. There is, in fact, activation of and discharge from the autonomic nervous system. These are accompanied by the physiological signs of tachycardia and/or palpitations, sweating, dryness of the mouth, nausea, vertigo, hyperventilation, tremors, and feelings of weakness. Prior to DSM-III clinicians simply labelled the individual as neurotic. Along with depression, anxiety is the other most common psychological disorder faced by those dealing with psychopathologies (95:187). Historically, anxiety disorders have been recognized by specific complaints that fall into the categories of panic attacks, phobias, and obsessions and compulsions. Most recently, generalized anxiety has been added.

Paradoxically, one assumes psychopathology if the lay person presents with these symptoms but expresses the belief that the athlete is not "psyched up" if he or she does *not* present. In fact, coaches everywhere spend considerable amounts of time, effort, and money to insure that these symptoms described above are not only present, but are emphasized and encouraged. While it is true that the athlete needs to be in a peak state of arousal if performance is to be optimum, no finite guidelines have been drawn to allow those working with the athlete to know what is "peak arousal" and what is "anxiety." If one were to discuss "double messages" this would be a classic place to begin. The athletic community has even gone so far as to suggest that once those symptoms stop appearing prior to competition, it is time to get out of the sport. The authors have never experienced competition, either as athletes or as coaches, in which those symptoms were not present, usually to an exaggerated degree. Rockwell brings out an interesting point by stating, "A major task the clinician faces is to identify anxiety and separate it from fear, alarm, panic, dread, etc. — each of which relates to clinical anxiety in some diagnostically and therapeutically important way (28:103)." Yet all of these are classified under anxiety disorders.

Tearnan and Telch described phobic reactions in three ways (1:163). Cognitively, the individual may report images or self-reverbalizations of expected negative consequences. Behaviorally, the most common reaction is avoidance of the feared situation. And lastly, the individual may experience a whole range of physiological responses in the presence of the stimuli including the normal nausea, dizziness, increased heart rate, choking, etc. The most widely accepted classification subdivides phobias into simple, social, and agoraphobia.

Many athletes have an intense fear of crowds. The fact that they are being watched every moment is terrifying. Upon examination of the definition in DSM-III (5:26) the essential feature of the agoraphobic is the marked fear of being alone or in a public place from which escape may be difficult (or in the athlete's case, impossible). How many times has one heard, "He's just young and inexperienced. He'll get over it." Perhaps that is so, but by the very definition of the term, that individual is agoraphobic. Since desensitization has proven effective in treatment of phobias, it is merely by coincidence that the phobic attacks subside as one gets more experience. The lay person is allowed to confess his or her problems and to get help, but the athlete is expected to "grow up."

Certainly, by the definition of social phobia, the athlete may also suffer from this overzealous scrutiny by others. Imagine trying to make a living at the very thing that triggers off phobic episodes.

The essential features of the panic attack are recurrent anxiety attacks that occur at unpredictable times. There is a sudden onset of intense apprehension, fear or terror, and sometimes feelings of impending doom. They can last from several minutes to several hours. Unlike phobias, the attacks do not occur in the presence of a particular stimulus. Generalized anxiety disorder is characterized by a continued anxious world for a period of at least one month. The differential diagnosis is the attacks present in panic disorder, even though an anxious state may exist between attacks. Clum and Picket emphasize, "The absence of an external stimulus does not eliminate the possibility of internal stimuli as elicitors of anxiety since internal stimuli are clearly suggested by the cognitive fears of 'dying, going crazy, or something uncontrolled' (1:201)." It may be a plausible explanation to look at the panic disorders and generalized anxiety state as learned behaviors in the athlete based upon phobic disorders.

Sturgis (1:251) discusses obsessive-compulsive behavior as ritualistic. The precise description of the obsessive-compulsive disorder that is spelled out in DSM-III (5:234) is that of the athlete prior to competition, "If I won the last game wearing my red wristband, then I'm going to continue to do so." Many athletes rehearse very complicated rituals prior to competition. And, as the literature describes, there is an impending feeling of doom if the ritual is not carried out precisely. Many of these individuals do not have the disorder present in any other aspects of their lives. Yet, because the sport is such a major part of her or his dynamic and social mindset, the problem should be considered significant. The sports media are laden with stories of particular rituals of various athletes. What is amusing to the lay public is a very serious matter to the athlete concerned. In many cases, the use of uppers (amphetamines) is more compulsion than anything else. The same is true with the use of anabolic steroids.

SOMATOFORM AND FACTITIOUS DISORDERS

Up to this point the concern has been primarily with the psychological side of behavior. Those areas mentioned so far were construed mainly as psychological problems. Attention now turns to a group of disorders in which the physiological complications are at least as important as the psychological. These disorders are linked to bodily processes in such a way as to produce genuine organic illnesses. Certainly, the physical symptoms require treatment in their own right. But a growing body of evidence indicates that disorders of this kind do not result solely from organic weakness nor from purely local tissue changes (95:304)."

The somatoform category consists of a class of disorders in which the physical symptoms play a prominent role. DSM-III (5:241) states that the essential features of this group of disorders are physical symptoms suggesting physical disorder for which there are no demonstrable organic findings. Unlike factitious disorders, the somatoform disorders are not under voluntary control (86:304). This group best illustrates that the mind and body are one and inseparable. In no other area outside of athletics are these disorders as significant. The athlete is paid, whether financially as with the professional or ego-stroking as with the amateur, for how his or her body performs. There are direct ties to the very livelihood of the individual. And for the athlete, what affects the mind definitely affects the body.

The somatization disorder features recurrent and multiple somatic complaints of several years duration for which medical attention has been sought. Complaints usually involve a system such as pseudoneurological, gastrointestinal, female reproductive, psychosexual, pain, and cardiopulmonary. For the athlete this can be totally incapacitating. Many others can perform at least work-oriented tasks, but because the body is the instrument of work for the athlete, the problem is quite acute. Very similar is the conversion disorder that is differentially diagnosed with a loss or major alteration in physical functioning that has no organic basis but is rather an expression of psychological conflict. For the athlete there may certainly be a full-blown episode of a conversion disorder but chances are it will be more subtle. Why, after hitting literally thousands of baseballs well, will a batter suddenly experience the inability to hit? Why can't a weight lifter who has done a specific weight with ease, suddenly not be able to match that lift? Why will a gymnast who has practiced a routine to perfection suddenly not be able to perform the dismount? Right now, no one has the answers. But if those symptoms fit the definition of a conversion disorder, which they do, why is it not treated as such?

As a group, one would have to say that athletes are some of the most severe hypochondriacs around. By definition of terms, the hypochondriac interprets physical signs or sensations as abnormal and believes that she or he is in the throws of a serious disease. The standard training room tongue-in-cheek comment is "tape an aspirin to his head and he'll be fine tomorrow." Anyone with training or coaching experience will verify the incidence of complaints. A serious question to be addressed at some point in the future of sports psychology is why this phenomenon exists.

Factitious disorders are distinguished from malingering by the fact that, though still under voluntary control, the individual is not "faking it" to avoid or control a situation. Behavior under voluntary control is used to pursue goals that are involuntarily adopted. Both factitious disorders and malingering are problems with deep psychological roots.

PERSONALITY DISORDERS

"It is interesting to note that in the field trials of DSM-III, personality disorders made up almost 50 percent of the psychiatric sample examined (1:495)." The key factor to remember when dealing with the athlete is the idea that the disorder causes both social and occupational impairment.

The paranoid personality disorder presents with pervasive and unwarranted suspiciousness and mistrust of people, hypersensitivity, and restricted affectivity. In athletics, the assessment of the problem lays with the rapidity at which someone can be replaced. Athletes are constantly in a position of having someone right over their shoulders ready to take over. And "immediately" means just that in sport. To the insecure individual this appears as a major problem. Many athletes become paranoid because of such a situation and the pressures they perceive as a result.

Perhaps no other area of personality disorders is fostered and developed more in athletes than the narcissistic disorder. As described in DSM-III (5:315) the essential feature is a grandiose sense of self-importance or uniqueness, preoccupation with fantasies of unlimited success, exhibitionistic need for constant attention, admiration, and feelings of entitlement. Now consider the manner in which an individual "learns" his or her narcissistic disorder. The example here, while fictitious in name, represents a very real situation that occurs to varying degrees in all segments of the athletic community.

Being the star of the football team and baseball team, John is handled with "kid gloves" in high school. The school newspaper tells him how good he is and how everyone depends upon him. The local press carries articles on him and his team weekly. Local athletic support groups have him as their guest at banquets to honor him. At school he is accorded all the rights and privileges of the BMOC. All the girls are impressed, all the underclassmen constantly seek his approval. He gets preregistered each semester with a special choice of instructors. When visiting officials come to the campus, he is pulled out of class to be introduced. In some cases, teachers may actually be told that he "does not" fail any classes and receives nothing lower than "C." When he is a senior, college recruiters wine and dine him. His name is plastered all over the newspapers prior to and after his decision on college. Just for running with a pigskin he receives a scholarship worth about $60,000 over four years, not to mention special meals, plane flights, special connections for a variety of uses, and special considerations from the faculty.

From college to the pros everything is magnified. His contract may be one of the best in the sport. He has access to anything he wants whenever he wants it. "Aw, shucks folks! It weren't really nothing" is a difficult posture to assume when everyone has told you that you are unique and have the potential for unlimited success that few can match. In athletics there exists the expression, "He read so many of his press clippings that he began to believe them." Athletes desperately need counseling to help adapt to the publicity arena in which they are placed.

Instability is pervasive in the Borderline disorder. It is interesting that many athletes develop borderline characteristics after having had a narcissistic disorder, which usually parallels their careers. Here again, there are very close similarities to the declining athlete and the DSM-III (5:322) criteria for Borderline Personality Disorder: Impulsivity or unpredictability in at least two areas that are potentially self-damaging-athletes involved in sex, gambling, substance abuse; a pattern of unstable and intense interpersonal relationships, many athletes start switching teams late in their careers; inappropriate, intense anger or lack of control, seen and allowed constantly in athletes; identity disturbance, for the athlete, if there are no more athletics, who am I? There is nothing else; affective instability, much more moody; physically self-damaging acts, going "all out" because its almost over; chronic feelings of emptiness and boredom, varies from one athlete to another. The point to be made here is one of situation. In many cases the athlete's world dictates these events, rather than being a psychopathology. But this certainly needs to be scrutinized more closely and from a new perspective.

The Passive Aggressive Disorder is quite prevalent in team sports where the individual is being asked to sacrifice for the good of the team. It is unacceptable and may even cost one an athletic career, to overtly resist. So once again, the "learned" behavior of the passive-aggressive disorder makes its appearance.

It needs to be emphasized here, again, that the authors are not attempting to compartmentalize all problems in alignment with DSM-III. The purpose of utilizing such a classification system is to allow for a common denominator to be used as a starting point for discussions and research. It is not being suggested that all athletes who encounter difficulties are suffering from a variety of psychopathologies, but close scrutiny needs to be given where none existed before.

Chapter Seven

THE ROLE OF THE SPORTS PSYCHOLOGIST

I N MOST CASES everyone working with the athlete has her or his time stretched to the maximum. A major consideration is to bring the sports psychologist into the picture as another tool toward improved performance, thereby allowing each professional a chance to maximize skills rather than trying to deal with an area in which they have little expertise. The tumbling block is the manner in which psychology is received by the public at large. Athletes are sensitive to public criticism, and should the public admonish athletes for seeking the expertise of a sports psychologist, the results would impair progress. The sports psychologist can serve many useful functions for the athlete, all resulting in the bottom line of improved performance.

Having recognized that these problems exist is a major first step. There are still those who would deny that any of these problems are specific to athletics, and that athletics are free from any of the symptoms described. Certainly the role of the sports psychologist working with the athlete encompasses more than the presentation of strategies for a small percentage. The clinician has an opportunity to effect significant changes in the triad of athletics. Because of the pressures of time, there is no one else for the marginally learning disabled athlete to turn to. And, thus, there exists a natural role to be filled. Each segment of the triad needs to be dealt with properly to achieve a positive balance.

In working with the individual, the clinician would have a significant degree of influence, primarily due to an ideal one-to-one situation. The rapport established and the trust maintained would be the cornerstones of improvement in performance. The sports psychologist would need to be supportive of the individual athlete in a number of areas. First and foremost, at the top of the priority list is performance. No matter how difficult, it needs to be emphasized that the clinician would not merely be a psychologist, but a *sports* psychologist. To the athlete with a learning disability, the psychologist who understands both the academic and performance aspects of the individual may be the first stable personal object in the person's athletic career. If the individual is aware of his or her academic deficiencies, then that knowledge needs to be transferred to the particular sport. If no prior knowledge of a disability existed, then the clinician must educate the person, and, at the same time, seek help from others concerned. As mentioned in the previous chapter, many problems that are present were created, whether directly or indirectly, by the learning disabilities. The vast majority of times, certainly due to the stress of athletics, those psychopathologies present become exacerbated. The sports psychologist would need to help the individual understand the dynamics of the overall situation. Those working closely with the learning disabled athlete also need to develop strategies, for enabling the athlete to cope and compensate.

In dealing with the second part of the triad, the team, a great deal of consideration needs to be given to establishing a positive relationship between the coach or coaching staff and the sports psychologist. Coaches need to understand that the approach to maximizing performance is a team approach, and that the sports psychologist is not at odds with the staff. A large potential for a polarity of ideas exists if the coach feels that he or she is being questioned for techniques that are somewhat deficient in dealing with a particular problem. The clinician needs not to interfere with the coach-player relationship, but rather to augment it. Teammates may be educated with regard to the disability so that rather than derogatory remarks, they may become watchful eyes to alert coaches and clinicians to communicative problems. In this fashion many difficulties can be resolved at an early stage. The purpose of the psychologist is not to act as a buffer, but to achieve the best possible interpersonal relationships for the team. By confronting potential problems and not disguising them, the socialization process is enhanced, generally resulting in an improved team performance.

The third segment of the triad is the crowd. A clinician can only indirectly influence crowd attitudes. Only through the process of education can the crowd understand the significance of a learning disability as it relates to sport. Part of the objectives of sports psychology should be to educate the lay public.

Reiterating previous ideas, if sport truly is 85-90 percent mental, then it is time that more emphasis was placed on this significant percentage. Being a part of mental preparedness, comprehending, coping, and compensating for learning disabilities is a scope of the athletic continuum to be dealt with by sports psychology.

Traditionally, athletics and psychology have been at opposite ends of a spectrum. At the infrared end was the image of the disciplined, godlike adonis who was impervious to pain or ridicule, while at the ultraviolet end was the empathic, bespectacled figure taking copious notes. The role of the sports psychologist is to glean the most appropriate aspects of each and bring them into focus in the sports arena. In this sense, learning disabilities may well serve as a means to bridge the gap. The academicians are satisfied because of previous research, norming, and reliability. The athletic community appreciates any progress towards improved performance. The new milieu is benefited by the strengths of each.

APPENDICES

Appendix A

APPLIED ATHLETIC DEFINITIONS OF LEARNING DISABILITY TERMS

"O" will be the operational athletic definition of the term, while "E" will be used to cite specific examples.

Auditory Mode Deficiencies

1. Acuity   O. The inability to hear sounds produced in athletics
E. Player constantly asks for signals to be repeated

2. Decoding   O. The inability to process plays or commands
E. Athlete has slow response time, but appears to hear plays and commands

3. Memory   O. The inability to remember coaching signals being given
E. Player cannot remember play or directions given by coach

4. Sequencing   O. Inability to remember a sequence of directions
E. An athlete can perform individual skills in isolation when given a verbal command but cannot sequence the pattern

5. Vocal   O. Similar to memory but in shorter time frame
E. When athlete is given verbal direction, he or she is unable to repeat directions back

Visual Mode Deficiencies

1. Acuity   O. Inability to see clearly
E. An athlete will spend extra time to focus on an object

2. Field   O. Part of the entire vision field is obscured
E. An athlete has no trouble seeing straight ahead but tends to lose objects to either side, above, or below

3. Coordination and Pursuit   O. Inability to follow and track objects
E. An athlete has difficulty pursuing an object or opponent

4. Figure-Ground   O. The inability to pick an object or opponent out of visual background
E. A player cannot find a particular opponent in a visual crowd

5. Form   O. The inability to detect proper position on others
E. Not remembering whether an opponent was right-handed or left-handed

6. Motor and Motor Memory   O. The inability to learn from visual examples such as films, diagrams, playbooks, etc.
E. A player cannot imitate proper technique after visual clues

7. Motor Integration   O. The athlete has poor spatial judgment
E. A player continually misjudges distances or size of objects and openings

Appendix B

YELLEN EVALUATION OF
ATHLETIC SKILLS (YEAS)

THE FOLLOWING checklist will provide the observer with an indication of weaknesses in any particular areas. The list should serve as a basis for communication between the observer and an expert in the area of compensation and remediation. It should be remembered that a one time incident does not constitute a deficiency and that the athlete needs to be observed without knowledge of or interference from the observer for the evaluation to be effective.

Auditory Mode Deficiency

circle one

Acuity

Says "What" frequently	Yes	No
Complains of not being able to hear directions	Yes	No
Has difficulty following directions	Yes	No
Looks at others for cues after verbal directions	Yes	No
Does not respond to signals from officials	Yes	No
Head turns to left or right when listening	Yes	No
Hearing examination Date:	Yes	No
Results:		

Decoding

Appears confused after verbal cues	Yes	No
Watches physical performance of others after verbal cues	Yes	No
Difficulty responding when directions are given	Yes	No
Subvocalizes after verbal cue	Yes	No

Memory

Difficulty following directions of coach or other athletes after verbal directions	Yes	No
Difficulty remembering verbal directions	Yes	No

Auditory Vocal

Difficulty carrying coaches verbal directions to others	Yes	No
Difficulty repeating back verbal directions	Yes	No

Sequencing

Difficulty remembering series of directions or order of events	Yes	No
Executes only initial verbal commands in a sequence	Yes	No
Executes only medial verbal commands in a sequence	Yes	No
Executes only final verbal commands in a sequence	Yes	No
Confuses order of skills from verbal commands	Yes	No

Visual Mode Deficiencies

Acuity

Squints in order to see	Yes	No
Complains of not being able to see clearly	Yes	No
Complains of glare	Yes	No
Turns head to align one eye or other to spot an object	Yes	No
Eye examination Date:	Yes	No
Results:		

Visual Coordination and Pursuit

Difficulty tracking an object through space	Yes	No
Difficulty following an opponent's actions	Yes	No
Difficulty hitting or striking an object while object is in motion	Yes	No

Field

Appears not to see objects to the extreme right	Yes	No
Appears not to see objects to the extreme left	Yes	No

Appears not to see objects below waist height	Yes	No
Appears not to see objects somewhat overhead	Yes	No

Figure Ground

Difficulty locating a teammate or opponent on the field or court	Yes	No
Difficulty locating the ball or other object with distractive visual background	Yes	No

Form

Difficulty remembering which hand opposing athlete uses for pitching, throwing, catching, etc.	Yes	No
Difficulty describing form of another athlete	Yes	No

Motor Memory

Difficulty remembering proper form after learning from coach, films, pictures, or other visual cues	Yes	No
Difficulty demonstrating to others	Yes	No

Motor Integration

Difficulty judging spatial distances between objects or players	Yes	No
Athlete continually states, "I thought I saw an opening"	Yes	No

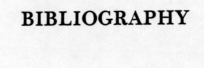

BIBLIOGRAPHY

Books

1. Adams, H.E. & Sutker, P.B. *Comprehensive Handbook of Psychopathology.* New York: Plenum Press, 1984.
2. Aiken, L.R. *Psychological Testing and Assessment.* Boston: Allyn and Bacon, 1982.
3. American Psychological Association. *Standards for Educational and Psychological Tests.* Washington, D.C.: APA, 1974.
4. A.P.A. *Diagnostic and Statistical Manual of Mental Disorders (DSM-III).* Washington, D.C.: APA, 1981.
5. _____ *Ethical Principles of Psychologists (1981 Rev.).* Washington, D.C.: APA, 1981.
6. _____ *Ethical Standards of Psychologists (Rev.).* Washington, D.C.: APA, 1977.
7. _____ *Standards for Providers of Psychological Services.* Washington, D.C.: APA, 1977.
8. Anderson, J.R. *Cognitive Skills and Their Aquisition.* New Jersey: Lawrence Erlbaum Associates, 1981.
9. Argyris, C. *Reasoning, Learning and Action.* San Francisco: Jossey-Bass, 1982.
10. Aronson, E. *The Social Animal (2nd Ed.).* San Francisco: W.H. Freeman, 1972.
11. Babad, E.Y., Birnbaum, M. & Benne, K.D. *The Social Self.* Beverly Hills, Ca.: Sage Publications, 1983.
12. Bloom, B.S., Hastings, J.T. & Madans, G.F. *Handbook of Formative and Summative Evaluation of Student Learning.* New York: McGraw-Hill, 1971.
13. Bricklin, B. & Bricklin, P. *Bright Child-Poor Grades.* New York: Delacorte Press, 1967.
14. Brutten, M., Richardson, S. & Manget. C *Something Wrong With My Child.* New York: Harcourt Brace Jovanovich, 1973.
15. Buros, O.D. (ed.). *The Eighth Mental Measurements Yearbook (Vol. 1 & 2).* Highland Park, N.J.: Grypton Press, 1978.
16. Bush, W.J. & Waugh, K.W. *Diagnosing Learning Disabilities.* Ohio: C.E. Merrill, 1976.
17. Bush, W.J. & Giles, M.T. *Aids to Psycholinguistics Teaching.* Ohio: C.E. Merrill, 1977.
18. Catell, R.B. *Personality and Motivation Structure and Measurement.* New York: Harcourt Brace & World, 1957.
19. Chomsky, N. *Rules and Representations.* New York: Columbia University Press, 1980.
20. Ciminero, A.R., Calhoun, K.S. & Adams, H.E. (eds.). *Handbook For Behavioral Assessment.* New York: John Wiley & Sons, 1976.

21. Clark, C. *Can't Read, Can't Write, Can't Talk Too Good Either.* New York: Walker & Co., 1973.
22. Cohen, G. *The Psychology of Cognition.* New York: Academic Press, 1977.
23. Cohen, H. *Connections.* Iowa: Iowa State U. Press, 1981.
24. Cronbach, L.J. *Essentials of Psychological Testing (3rd Ed.).* New York: Harper and Row, 1970.
25. Crackshank, W.M., Morse, W.C. & Johns, J.S. *Learning Disabilities.* New York: Syracuse Press, 1980.
26. Cavison, G.C. & Neale, J.M. *Abnormal Psychology.* New York: John Wiley & Sons, 1978.
27. Doehring, D.G. Trites, R.C., Putel, P.G. & Fiedorowicz, C.A. *Reading Disabilities.* New York: Academic Press, 1981.
28. Donlon, P.T. & Rockwell, D.A. *Psychiatric Disorders: Diagnosis and Treatment.* Maryland: R.J. Brady, 1982.
29. Downie, N.M. & Heath, R.W. *Basic Statistical Methods (3rd Ed.).* New York: Harper and Row, 1970.
30. d'Ydewalle, G. & Lens, W. *Cognition in Human Motivation and Learning.* New Jersey: Lawrence Erlbaum Associates, 1981.
31. Ellis, A.W. (ed.). *Normality and Pathology in Cognitive Functions.* New York: Academic Press, 1982.
32. Exner, J.E. *The Rorschach: A Comprehensive System.* New York: John Wiley & Sons, 1974.
33. Fields, R.R.J. & Horowitz, R.J. *Psychology and Professional Practice.* Westport, Conn.: Quorom Books, 1982.
34. Fodor, J.D. *The Language of Thought.* New York: Crowell, 1975.
35. Freeman, J. *The Politics of Women's Liberation.* New York: David McKay, 1975.
36. Freeman, S.W. *Does Your Child Have A Learning Disability?* Springfield, Ill.: Charles C Thomas, 1974.
37. Frostig, M. & Horne, D. *Teacher's Guide: The Frostig Program for the Development of Visual Perception (Re. Ed.).* Chicago: Follet Ed. Corp., 1974.
38. Goethals, G.R. & Worchel, S. *Adjustment and Human Relations.* New York: Alfred Knopf, 1981.
39. Golden, C.J. *Clinical Interpretation of Objective Psychological Tests.* New York: Grune & Stratton, 1979.
40. Goldman-Eisler, F. *Psycholinguistics.* London: Academic Press, 1968.
41. Gregg, L.W. *Cognition in Learning and Memory.* New York: John Wiley & Sons, 1974.
42. _____ *Knowledge and Cognition.* New York: John Wiley & Sons, 1974.
43. Harari, H. & Kaplan, R.M. *Social Psychology.* Monterey, CA: Brooks/Cole Pub. Co., 1982.
44. Holt, J. *The Underachieving School.* New York: Delta Books, 1970.
45. Hunt, S. & Hilton, J. *Individual Development and Social Experience.* London: George, Allen & Unwin, 1981.
46. Jarvik, M.E. (ed.). *Psychopharmacology in the Practice of Medicine.* New York: Appleton-Century-Crofts, 1977.

47. Johnson, O.G. *Tests and Measurements in Child Development: Handbook II*. San Fancisco: Jossey-Bass, 1976.
48. Kaplan, S. & Kaplan, R. *Cognition and Environment*. New York: Praeger, 1981.
49. Kazdin, A.E., Belack, A.S. & Hersen, M. *New Perspectives in Abnormal Psychology*. New York: Oxford U. Press, 1980.
50. Kephart, N.C. *The Slow Learner in the Classroom. (Ed. 2)*. Columbus, Ohio: C.E. Merrill, 1971.
51. Kinsbourne M. & Caplan, P. *Children's Learning and Attention Problems*. Boston: Little Brown, 1979.
52. Kranes, J.E. *The Hidden Handicap*. New York: Simon & Schuster, 1980.
53. Kreitler, H. & Kreitler, S. *Cognitive Orientation and Behavior*. New York: Springer, 1976.
54. Lawson, C.A. *Brain Mechanisms and Human Learning*. Boston: Houghton Mifflin, 1967.
55. Luria, A.R. *Cognitive Development*. Mass.: Harvard U. Press, 1976.
56. Manis, E. *Cognitive Processes*. California: Wadworth, 1966.
57. Mercer, C.D. *Students With Learning Disabilities*. Columbus: C.E. Merrill, 1983.
58. Mischel, W. *Pesonality and Assessment*. New York: John Wiley & Sons, 1968.
59. McNeil, E.B. & Rubin, Z. *The Psychology of Being Human*. San Francisco: Canfield, 1977.
60. McReynolds, P. *Advances in Psychological Assessment (Vols. 1 & 2)*. Palo Alto: Science & Behavior Books, 1968 & 1971.
61. _____ *Advances in Psychological Assessment (Vols. 3, 4, & 5)*. San Francisco: Jossey-Bass Pub., 1975, 1978, 1981.
62. National Institute on Drug Abuse. *Frequently Prescribed and Abused Drugs*. Maryland: NIDA, 1980.
63. Neal, A.G. *Social Psychology*. Mass.: Addison-Wesley Pub. Co., 1983.
64. Oskamp, S. *Attitudes and Opinions*. Englewood Cliffs, N.J.: Prentice-Hall, 1977.
65. Osman, B.B. *Learning Disabilities, A Family Affair*. New York: Warner Books, 1979.
66. _____ *No One To Play With*. New York: Random House, 1982.
67. Phillips, J.L. *The Social Skills Basis of Psychopathology*. New York: Grune & Stratton, 1978.
68. Phillips, J.L. *Piaget's Theory: A Primer*. San Francisco: W.H. Freeman, 1981.
69. Pribram, K.A. *Languages of the Brain*. New Jersey: Prentice-Hall, 1971.
70. Posner, M.I. *Cognition*. Illinois: Scott, Foresman & Co., 1973.
71. Rochester, S.R. & Martin, J.G. *Crazy Talk: A Study of the Discourse of Schizophrenic Speakers*. New York: Plenum Press, 1979.
72. Sahakian, W.S. *History and Systems of Social Psychology*. Washington: Hemisphere, 1982.
73. Sattler, J.M. *Assessment of Children's Intelligence*. Philadelphia: W.B. Saunders, 1974.
74. Schiff, W. *Perception: An Applied Approach*. Boston: Houghton Mifflin, 1980.
75. Selye, H. *Stress Without Distress*. Philadelphia: J.B. Lippincott, 1974.
76. Sprott, R.L. *Age, Learning Ability and Intelligence*. New York: Van Nostrand Reinhold, 1980.

77. Stevens, S.H. *The Learning Disabled Child: Ways That Parents Can Help.* N.C.: John F. Blair, 1980.
78. Stringer, P. (ed.). *Confronting Social Issues: Applications of Social Psychology, (Vols. I & II).* London: Academic Press, 1982.
79. Sundberg, N.D. *Assessment of Personality.* Englewood Cliffs, N.J.: Prentice-Hall, 1977.
80. Swenson, W.M., Pearson, J.S. & Osborne, L. *An MMPI Sourcebook: Basic Item, Scale & Pattern Date on 50,000 Medical Patients.* Minneapolis: Minnesota Press, 1973.
81. Terman, L.M. & Merrill, M.A. *Stanford Binet Intelligence Scale: Manual For The Third Revision* Boston: Houghton Mifflin, 1973.
82. Thain, W.S., Castro, G. & Peterson, A. *Normal and Handicapped Children.* Mass.: P.S.G., 1980.
83. Thomas, A. & Chess, S. *Temperament and Development.* New York: Brunner/Mazel, 1977.
84. Thorne, B.M. *Indroductory Statistics for Psychology.* North Scituate, Mass.: Duxbury Press, 1980.
85. Tighe, T.J. *Modern Learning Theory: Foundations and Fundamentals.* New York: Oxford U. Press, 1982.
86. Turner, S.M. & Hersen, M. *Adult Psychopathology and Diagnosis.* New York: John Wiley & Sons, 1984.
87. Underwood, B.J., Duncan, C.P., Spence, J.T. & Cotton, J.W. *Elementary Statistics.* New York: Appleton-Century-Crofts, 1954.
88. Ungerleider, D.F. *Reading, Writing, and Rage.* Rolling Hills Estates: Jalmar Press, 1984.
89. Usdin, E. & Forrest, I. *Psychotherapeutic Drugs.* New York: Marcel Dekker, 1976.
90. Valett, R.E. *The Remediation of Learning Disabilities.* Belmont, CA: Fearon, 1967.
91. von Cranach, M., Kalbermatten, V. & Gugler, K.I.B. *Goal-Directed Action.* London: Academic Press, 1982.
92. Wagner, R. *Dyslexia and Your Child.* New York: Harper & Row, 1971.
93. Walk, R.D. & Pick, H.L. *Intersensory Perception and Sensory Integration.* New York: Plenum Press, 1981.
94. Wechsler, D. *The Measurement and Appraisal of Adult Intelligence (4th).* Baltimore: Williams and Wilkins, 1958.
95. Wender, P.H. & Klein, D.F. *Mind, Mood and Medicine.* New York: Farrar-Strauss-Giroux, 1981.
96. White, R.W. & Watt, N.F. *The Abnormal Personality,* New York: John Wiley & Sons, 1981.
97. Whitmore, J.R. *Giftedness, Conflict and Underachievement.* Boston: Allyn & Bacon, 1980.
98. Willerman, L. *The Psychology of Individual and Group Differences.* San Francisco: W.H. Freeman, 1979.
99. Yalom, I.D. *Theory and Practice of Group Psychotherapy.* New York: Basic Books, 1975.
100. Zimmerman, I.L. & Woo-San, J.M. *Clinical Interpretation of the Wechsler Adult Intelligence Scale.* New York: Grune & Stratton, 1973.

Clinical Instruments

101. Bender Visual Motor Gestalt. Western Psychological Services, Los Angeles.
102. Minnesota Multiphasic Personality Inventory (MMPI). The Psychological Corp., New York.
103. Rorschach Inkblot Test. The Psychological Corp., New York.
104. Thematic Apperception Test (TAT). The Psychological Corp., New York.
105. Wechsler Adult Intelligence Scale (WAIS). The Psychological Corp., New York.
106. Wechsler Intelligence Scale for Children-Revised (WISC-R). The Psychological Corp., New York.
107. Wide Range Achievement Test (WRAT). The Psychological Corp., New York.
108. 16 Personality Factor Questionnaire (16PF). Institute for Personality and Ability Testing, Champaign, Ill.

INDEX